A
RELATIONSHIP
FOR A
LIFETIME

Also by Kelly E. Johnson, M.D.

Relationship Problem Solver

Hay House Titles of Related Interest

BOOKS

Getting Unstuck, by Joy Browne

The Love Book, by John Randolph Price

Rising in Love: *Opening Your Heart in All Your Relationships,* by Alan Cohen

Secrets of Attraction: *The Universal Laws of Love, Sex, and Romance,* by Sandra Anne Taylor

AUDIO PROGRAMS

Dr. Phil Getting Real: *Lessons in Life, Marriage, and Family,* by Dr. Phil McGraw

The Romance Angels, by Doreen Virtue, Ph.D.

CARD DECK

MarsVenus Cards, a 50-Card Deck by John Gray

All of the above are available at your local bookstore, or may be ordered by visiting:

Hay House USA: www.hayhouse.com
Hay House Australia: www.hayhouse.com.au
Hay House UK: www.hayhouse.co.uk
Hay House South Africa: orders@psdprom.co.za

A RELATIONSHIP FOR A LIFETIME

Everything You Need to Know
to Create a Love
That Lasts

KELLY E. JOHNSON, M.D.

HAY HOUSE, INC.
Carlsbad, California
London • Sydney • Johannesburg
Vancouver • Hong Kong

Copyright © 2001 by Kelly E. Johnson

Published and distributed in the United States by: Hay House, Inc., P.O. Box 5100, Carlsbad, CA 92018-5100 • *Phone:* (760) 431-7695 or (800) 654-5126 • *Fax:* (760) 431-6948 or (800) 650-5115 • www.hayhouse.com • *Published and distributed in Australia by:* Hay House Australia Pty. Ltd., 18/36 Ralph St., Alexandria NSW 2015 • *Phone:* 612-9669-4299 • *Fax:* 612-9669-4144 • www.hayhouse.com.au • *Published and distributed in the United Kingdom by:* Hay House UK, Ltd. • Unit 62, Canalot Studios • 222 Kensal Rd., London W10 5BN • *Phone:* 44-20-8962-1230 • *Fax:* 44-20-8962-1239 • www.hayhouse.co.uk • *Published and distributed in the Republic of South Africa by:* Hay House SA (Pty), Ltd., P.O. Box 990, Witkoppen 2068 • *Phone/Fax:* 27-11-706-6612 • orders@psdprom.co.za • *Distributed in Canada by:* Raincoast • 9050 Shaughnessy St., Vancouver, B.C. V6P 6E5 • *Phone:* (604) 323-7100 • *Fax:* (604) 323-2600

Editorial supervision: Jill Kramer • *Design:* Charles McStravick

Library of Congress Cataloging-in-Publication Data

Johnson, Kelly E.
    A relationship for a lifetime: everything you need to know to create a love that lasts / Kelly E. Johnson
        p. cm.
    ISBN 1-56170-809-7 (tradepaper)
    1. Man-woman relationships. 2. Marriage. I. Title.

HQ801.J593 2001
306.7–dc21

                                        2001024050

                ISBN 13: 978-1-56170-809-3
                ISBN 10: 1-56170-809-7

        08 07 06 05   7 6 5 4
        1st printing, October 2001
        4th printing, January 2005

            Printed in Canada

*This book is dedicated
with all my heart and love
to my wife, Betsy,
who completed my life and showed
me how to love unconditionally.*

*To my parents,
who have always provided the foundation
and security for me to succeed.*

*And in memory of my grandparents,
the most generous and giving people
I have ever known.*

Contents

PART II: RELATIONSHIP THERAPY

Please note:
All of the stories and case studies in this book are true.
All names have been changed for confidentiality purposes.

Acknowledgments

I COULD NOT HAVE WRITTEN THIS BOOK WITHOUT THE HELP and support of many wonderful people. They each have contributed joy to my life, and I extend my deepest gratitude to all of them.

I thank my wife, Betsy, for her love and positive outlook on life, which has certainly made me feel less vulnerable as I embark on a new career path. I always know that she stands beside me and that our bond truly is a relationship for life. Any of us would be fortunate to find such a loyal and accepting partner.

To my parents, Edward and Patricia Johnson, I give a huge thank you, although this cannot even begin to pay them back for the mountain of love they have given to me. Everyone needs a safety net in life, and they are mine. I certainly believe that God had a plan for me to be with them. They also set a great example of how two people should love each other.

A big round of thanks goes to my extended family, all of whom accepted me into their lives from day one. They have always made me feel comfortable and valued as an important presence in the family. I give heartfelt appreciation to Jennifer and Jim Boerger, Bob and Betsy Jennings, Jim and Kathy Gresham, and Dave and Kim O'Donoghue. They have all helped me become a better person.

I give thanks to Dr. Joel Mostow, my business partner in psychiatry, who is one of the smartest and most responsible physicians I know. He's been there for me in many different ways and has challenged me to become a better listener and clinician. He also just happens to be one of my best friends. I will always treasure our connection.

I also thank my other business partner in life, Karen Hand, who co-hosts our radio show, "Private Lives." She is absolutely the best personality that I've ever heard on the radio, and she is the true energy and passion of our show. She has been incredibly supportive in helping me develop communication skills, as well as turning me on to the whole field of relationship self-help.

I thank all of the people who have been my teachers throughout my life. From grade school through my psychiatric training, I've been fortunate to receive an outstanding education. Teachers are the real heroes in our society and deserve more recognition. This book is the product of many of the concepts about life and relationships that I've learned from them. I can only hope to give back to you a little of what I received from them.

A huge thanks goes to all of the folks who have allowed me to help them over the years. It requires a great leap of faith to share the innermost details of your life with someone else. Yet I am the better for it—my patients and the listeners of the radio show have changed my life in positive ways.

To all of the people at Hay House, I cannot express my gratitude enough for your support and positive energy. You all have truly been a beacon of light as you have welcomed me into your family. A special heartfelt thanks to Danny Levin, who has been my guide and friend throughout the last year. His involvement with this project has made the difference for me. He is simply one of the nicest and kindest people whom I have ever met. Much gratitude goes to Jill Kramer and Shannon Littrell for helping shape this manuscript with their tireless editing.

Finally, to you, the reader, I give thanks that you are allowing me to become a part of your life. I sincerely hope that you enjoy this book and use it to make a difference in your relationship.

Introduction

ACKSTAGE, I STOOD ALONE, STARING INTENTLY AT A small television monitor as it flickered in the dark, analyzing the people on the screen just as if they were sitting in my psychiatric office. Yet this was no psychotherapy session—these individuals' most intimate and embarrassing relationship issues weren't only being exposed to me, but to an audience of millions across the nation. I could hear the yelling and crying from the set of the show, actually only a few feet away. With each guest's revelations of cheating, lying, and self-destructive behavior, the studio audience roared.

This was big-time American television, with incredibly high stakes for everyone involved. The syndication company, the host of the show, and the guests themselves all had a lot riding on each juicy confession and confrontation—huge ratings would be the ultimate payoff. These daytime TV talk shows are indeed our country's newest form of "relationship therapy."

In a few moments, my purpose would be clear. One of the producers would say, "Dr. Johnson, we're ready for you," and I'd confidently stride onto the set and into your living room. My job, as the expert, was to make some sense out of the mayhem and misery revealed over the past hour. All of the sordid relationship scenarios had unfolded before me, and it was time for me to deliver the goods, so to speak. I usually try to focus on the one or two guests who appear the most disturbed and who have generated the most animosity, as people like this always claim to have their act together, but their lives are usually complete disasters. Then I ready myself and hope for the best. Whatever happens on that stage is generally shown unedited on television—it's a pressure cooker, but at the same time, oddly energizing. Every word and mannerism of each person on the stage is up for scrutiny by the viewers. The adrenaline of everybody in that studio is sky high, as "ordinary" people do the most outrageous things.

But there's the chance that I could stand above the fray, delivering words of wisdom and enlightenment designed to quickly repair years of terrible relationships and hurtful behaviors. I'm usually given a few minutes at the end of each show to make a diagnosis and tell America what's wrong with the participants. The audience will clap when I say something that's on target; and some guests will insult me and insist that I don't know what I'm talking about when I call them out on their dysfunctional coping skills. Being professional *and* giving advice in a sound bite is the name of the game.

The Real Problems of Real People

I'm one of the few psychiatrists in the country who's been able to appear regularly in the media over the years—

on several daytime talk shows and as the co-host of a radio show. As a result of these appearances, I'm known as a "relationship expert"—someone who can supposedly fix even the worst disasters and cure a lifetime of pain in just a few minutes. I can honestly say that I've pretty much seen it all, having done shows with such themes as adultery, family squabbles, sexual addictions, and women who continue to profess their "love" to men who regularly beat them up, just to name a few.

And this is just the tip of the iceberg. No private matter has been taboo—although my weekly radio show is called "Private Lives," once someone calls me on the airwaves, their life is up for public scrutiny. Like it or not, that's the way it is now. These TV and radio shows are here to stay, because we, the public, demand it. If we were able to stop watching or listening, the revenue streams would dry up and the shows would soon be pulled off the air. But we're alternately fascinated and repulsed by these *real* people with *real* relationship problems, all of whom exhibit really inadequate ways of dealing with life. We're voyeurs, entertained by the high drama of common people fighting it out every day in a very public venue.

When I first started talking openly on the radio in Chicago several years ago about relationships in an "anything goes" radio format, I certainly received a fair share of criticism, both from the public and from some of my colleagues. I then started to make the television rounds, and the criticism intensified. Several of my peers cried foul, insisting that the people on these shows had to be "fakes"—actors hired to portray people in unbelievable situations that could never happen in real life. They further claimed that there's simply no way to truly help anyone in just a few minutes on TV or radio, something you may also believe.

I'll grant you that there's some validity to this argument, but I know from firsthand experience that the people on that stage with me are real, flown in from all over the country for their 15 minutes of fame. What's amazing to me is that, by and large, they're not "freaks," but just some average folks who want to find meaning in their lives or perhaps get a few answers. Maybe they're going about it the wrong way, but their pain is real. They have families, jobs, hopes, and dreams that may have been shattered by their own doing, since most of the time, they're their own worst enemies. Maybe it's a cathartic experience for them to vent their lifetime of anger in one big explosion on television. But regardless of the reason why they choose to share their difficulties with us, one thing is quite clear: *Most of these people have no clue whatsoever why they do the things they do in their personal relationships.* They have no basic understanding of their relationship choices, and consequently, they'll be destined to a lifetime of unhappiness, pain, and difficult love affairs.

These people are out of control, angry beyond belief that their lives haven't turned out the way they once envisioned, and they blame anyone but themselves. After the show ends, most of them will return to their hometowns and continue to self-destruct.

Sadly, this reflects the current state of many relationships—the media only shows what already exists out there. Here's the newest attitude about relationships: *It's not my fault that I literally destroyed everything—someone else made me do it!* These people on TV probably won't achieve true happiness because they simply won't take the time to thoughtfully reflect on their own behaviors and emotions. They lack this vital character trait, and think that anger and finger pointing will somehow achieve a positive result.

Jerry Springer has been lambasted in the mainstream media for a number of years, but I will say this for him and his show: If anything positive is to be gained from watching his circus of dysfunction, it's that the show teaches us the *absolute wrong way* to go about managing our emotions and our lives! Carefully notice the approach to relationships that his guests take . . . and then do the exact opposite. There seems to be no pretense of helping anyone, other than Jerry's brief message at the end that implores you to do something entirely different from the people on his show. Also be aware that the violence and anger perpetrated on that stage is only the outward manifestation of each guest's deep feelings of insecurity, shame, and resentment. When you think of it this way, it almost seems very sad and pathetic. *People who don't understand themselves will continue to fight and break up*; that is, they'll continue to do what they know.

Ironically, many years ago it used to be almost shameful to air your "dirty laundry" with anyone but your significant other or your psychiatrist. Problems were worked out very discreetly and privately, as it was embarrassing to admit a relationship failure. People did divorce, but they did so quietly. Relationships ended, but you couldn't tell it from the "happy endings" on most TV shows. You always knew that even if the couple argued their way through the entire program, at the end they would somehow find a way to make up and keep the relationship intact for at least another week. People on TV were never shown reading self-help books, taking quizzes in *Cosmopolitan*, or going to the marital therapist because their relationship was in total disarray.

But then something changed. The reality set in that a lot of people in relationships simply weren't living in

Pleasantville. The skyrocketing divorce rate in our country couldn't be ignored any longer. As of this writing, *over half of all marriages* will break up and end in divorce. I will expand more on this later, but think about that for a moment. You have a better chance of enduring a painful relationship than one that lasts forever. Even if you are one of the lucky ones who will stay with your partner, there's an even greater chance that one of you will commit adultery.

The reality is that most of us can't get along well enough to honor our marriage or commitment vows. When the road gets bumpy, we either immediately call up our friendly divorce lawyer, or we begin an affair that not only ruins our own life, but that of our family as well. We become mean-spirited and disrespectful to our partner, and then the relationship is pretty much over. It's not in vogue to do the tough work to keep things together.

You Have the Power to Change

I realize that you'll probably never be on television airing your life's problems. In fact, you've most likely seen the shows I've been speaking of and have ridiculed the guests. If you're like me, you may have been shocked by these people and their lives. It's also tempting to think that you have absolutely nothing in common with these people because they seem so screwed up. But I'll bet that there's one thing that's similar: *They're unhappy with their past and current relationship choices, and so are you.* They may yell and scream on TV, but you suffer silently. Moreover, if you don't ever make an effort to understand the origins of your relationship choices either, you may repeat the same mistakes over and over, just as they do.

This book will challenge you to make a change in your own life and understand your behavior in a way that guests on daytime talk shows don't. You can't stop *them* from crashing, but you certainly can develop the power to *change yourself.*

So what are the things that you can expect to gain from following the principles that I have carefully outlined within these pages? At the outset, you may be skeptical, thinking that this will degenerate into a bunch of psychobabble or nonsense that can't be applied on a practical level. Let me assure you up front that I intend for this to be a very different experience for you, as we delve into some crucial concepts that to my knowledge have *never* been tackled in a mainstream self-help book. I believe that you could read 1,000 books on how men and women communicate differently, or on how to spark some romance, but these books will *not* lead to a fundamental change in the quality of your relationship if it's in serious danger of dissolving. If you've engaged in a string of unsatisfying relationships and can't figure out why you chose the wrong people, or if you're unhappy and on the verge of breaking up, you've got to *understand why* you're in such desperate straits.

There are definite reasons for the relationship choices you make in life, and these don't come out of nowhere. You can't avoid the following reality any longer: *These choices are a direct result of your past, your previous experiences in life, and what you have seen and heard.* This concept may be new to you, but it's the premise that underlies the rest of this book. In fact, it's also one of the most important ideas that you'll ever be asked to consider!

Your road to *self-discovery* doesn't have to be overwhelming and frightening, but instead could be looked at as a wonderful opportunity to improve your odds at creating a great relationship. Look at the alternative: Remaining uninformed about your own psychology is like going into the big game with only half the equipment you need to win. You may get lucky once in a while, but chances are that you'll walk away feeling defeated, wondering what you did wrong.

In the process of objectively analyzing your relationships, you'll by necessity learn a great deal about *you*. My goal is to help you understand what makes you tick, and know why you do certain things in the course of a relationship. Obviously these aren't easy questions to answer, but I don't know of a more effective way for you to grow as a person. It's time to face this other undeniable relationship reality: *You will have great difficulty finding peace and happiness in* any *personal relationship if you don't have your own act together!*

I can't tell you the number of people whom I've counseled over the years who wonder why their relationships fall apart, and yet haven't put one ounce of energy into understanding themselves and their life choices. Maybe they, like you, have been too proud to walk into the local therapist's office and shout, "I need help!" Maybe they've been talked out of it because their partner is from the old school and simply thinks that any type of self-examination or therapy is a total waste of time. Maybe they've read a bunch of self-help books that promise the "quick fix," but never get to the root of the problem. Well, I'm here to tell you that *without outside help, most relationships in trouble won't improve over time.* Don't let anyone fool you into believing otherwise. Don't fall into the trap of accepting mediocrity in your relationships and life. You certainly deserve to be happy as much as anyone else on this planet, but achieving your personal nirvana may involve some sweat and hard work. I used to be envious of those who I thought were lucky enough to stumble upon a wonderful relationship. Then one day I realized that this wasn't just luck—these people had done their homework in order to *create* the good things in their lives.

What I will offer to you in this book is the opportunity to do some *relationship therapy*—just by reading this material. In Part I, we'll look at the realities that apply to any and all love relationships. Each chapter will discuss a different "Relationship Reality" that should be accepted as part of your life. These are *givens* that exist no matter what type of relationship you create or how long you've been in that relationship. There's some vital information in these chapters, so read carefully and slowly.

Then, in Part II, we'll develop a *real* way to approach your relationship that's not based on the latest set of "rules" or the fad of the moment. I don't make many guarantees, but I will make one promise to you: If you're the least bit interested in making sense of your life experience thus far, you can't afford *not* to know these things! This is because the principles that I describe are *universal*, and apply whether you're in the throes of marital problems, divorce, infidelity, or unhappy dating. Even if you just aren't happy with the level of intimacy and communication in an otherwise good relationship, or your partner just drives you crazy, you'll benefit from some introspection.

Why am I so confident that you'll emerge as a changed person at the end of this book? It's simple—*everything that I'll share with you is exactly what we would discuss if you were sitting in my office,* engaging in therapy aimed at solving your relationship woes. As opposed to some other authors, I'm a psychiatrist who conducts actual relationship therapy with actual patients. There's *no* substitute for *sound psychological principles* that help you navigate your relationships. The concepts are proven to work, and have been used by professional therapists for years! So, like anything else in life, if you stick with it and push to the end, you'll notice a fundamental change in the way you think about yourself and your personal relationships.

So are you ready for a journey that could literally change your life? I hope that you are, but please realize that there's no "magic" to any of the answers I have to offer. I have no tricks up my sleeve, because I believe that you don't need any more illusions thinly disguised as relationship advice. You *do* need to develop the talent to become your own relationship expert. You can then be part of the solution and not part of the problem. You can achieve greatness in all of your personal relationships. The only question is whether you're willing to accept the realities about life and relationships that apply to every single one of us.

The cold, hard truth is this: *Successful people have taken the time to understand themselves so that they don't continue to make the same relationship mistakes.* They've mastered certain concepts about relationships in general and about themselves. They know that there's a *reason* for every single thing that they do in their lives.

Likewise, there's a reason why *you've* been attracted to certain people. There's a reason why these relationships did or didn't work for you. There's a reason why you've stayed with someone who doesn't make you happy. There's a reason why you've experienced infidelity, sexual problems, a lack of communication, or a myriad of other issues that end relationships. There's a reason why you may push someone away who could be a wonderful, loving life partner. There's a reason why your friends may have terrific relationships and you don't. There's a reason why you're alone right now, struggling after a divorce. This list could go on and on. Why not take the time to make sense of your experiences? Uncover these reasons, and you'll dramatically heighten the peace and joy you experience in all of your life relationships.

Come with me, and take the challenge to truly know yourself. Think of this as a gift to yours truly, an investment that will yield many happy returns.

PART I

The Reality of Your Relationship

The Relationship Realities

1. You are the creator of your relationship. It's a valuable possession that you own.

2. There is no set of relationship rules that you must follow. The work to understand your relationship is what's really important.

3. You must stop living in a fantasy world, just hoping that things will somehow change for the better in your relationships. Change will only occur if you *do something*. Take action and set your limits.

4. What you allow to happen in your relationship is what you're going to get. Defining what you need and claiming your power is a critical step in maximizing your happiness.

5. If you need to work really hard early in the relationship, then there may be big problems down the road. Get off the relationship roller coaster.

6. If you need something, the only way to get it will be to tell your partner. No one can read your mind.

7. The right timing is a crucial factor in determining whether a particular relationship will progress. Just because *you're* ready doesn't mean that a potential partner will move at the same speed.

8. A relationship with a shaky foundation will probably not get better with the addition of children.

9. You can't always get what you want in any relationship. Great relationships happen as a result of both partners developing selfless attitudes.

10. Serious relationship problems require therapy. There's no substitute for a process that helps you understand the root of your relationship conflicts. Relationships aren't simple, and there are no simple answers.

CHAPTER 1

You Are the Creator of Your Relationships

WELCOME TO YOUR LIFE.
Allow me to introduce you to yourself. I want you to stop whatever else you've planned for the day and take this challenge. Take a look at your partner, job, home, children, and all of the people with whom you have a personal relationship. Then realize a fundamental truth about all of these things: *You created every single one of them!*

This is what you've done in the world. Do you like what you see?

Or are you desperately unhappy, secretly wishing that someone else would make it better? Maybe you've fooled yourself into believing that your time will come, and if you just wait long enough, everything will "magically" change. Well, I've got news for you—your time is *now*. Success in your personal relationships will be measured by how you choose to spend this precious time—when you become an active participant in your own life.

So it's time for a wake-up call. I'd like you to repeat out loud the following statement, no matter how uncomfortable it may sound to you:

> *"I'm a creator. My relationships are a direct result of the choices that I've made. I'll only be able to achieve true happiness when I take personal responsibility for my life decisions. If a change needs to occur, I'm the only one with the power to effect it. If I continue to be unhappy in a relationship, it's because I'm allowing this unhappiness."*

Say these words over a few times. Concentrate and focus on what this means for your life—how does it feel to you? Does it feel awkward to admit that your relationships can only happen as you choose? If you're like most people, it's usually easier to blame someone else for your life's failures. Don't get me wrong—I'm not trying to be overly critical of a coping skill that most of us have raised to an art form. But the fact is that before we can go any further, you must begin to take ownership of your life relationships. You're not a child anymore and can't depend on someone else to blaze a path for you. My father would have put it more succinctly: "Wake up and smell the coffee!"

I was describing this "concept of creation" to one of my patients once, and he proclaimed, "Reality stinks!" To which I countered that his relationships weren't all that good, but they were what they were. His personal feeling on the subject didn't change the stark reality of his life, which was that he was mired in an unhappy marriage and wasn't doing a thing about it except to complain to me. No one had forced him to marry a woman whom he didn't love, and he certainly wasn't being held hostage to stay with her. Yet, like millions of other people, he'd never bothered to understand his own motives, and consequently stayed in an unfulfilling relationship. Moreover, he had a laundry list of complaints about his wife, consisting of things that he didn't get from her. But did he ever tell her his feelings? No, because in his own words, "She's just supposed to know what I want." This relationship was doomed—they divorced several months later, mainly because he was only along for the ride. He never grasped the crucial concept that this was also his relationship to make or break, and that he had a major part in causing its demise. He chose to let the relationship get to a point of no return by doing nothing for years except suffer in silence. He refused to face reality.

The Concept of Personal Ownership

You own many things. I've asked hundreds of people over the years to list all of their important possessions, from top to bottom, and they all invariably come up with similar lists. Houses, cars, furniture, stocks, and other material goods usually rank highly. Then I tell them that they've overlooked the number-one valuable commodity in their life. They usually look at me with a blank stare, because the majority of us don't ever think of our personal relationship as something to be possessed. Here, then, is the first **Relationship Reality.**

> *You are the creator of your relationship.*
> *It's a valuable possession that you own.*

Why is it so difficult to accept the truth that you're the owner of a relationship? After all, you initially saw something that you wanted, took steps to obtain it, and then made a decision to keep it in your life. Sounds like a possession to me. But there's something inherently more complex about a marriage or committed relationship that makes it harder to quantify. Maybe it's because there's no definite point when you actually "buy" a relationship. Or perhaps it has something to do with the notion of love and romance, as most of us get caught up in the idea that we "share" a special relationship, and it would appear greedy to claim ownership. But whatever the reason, I've run across few people who enthusiastically embrace the idea of seeing themselves as the owner of a relationship. It's easier to just "let it happen" and hope for a good result. Avoiding the thought that you're responsible for the relationship also allows you to avoid accepting the blame when something goes seriously wrong.

In addition, being an owner carries with it the responsibility of learning about your product. Unfortunately, you've probably never read a set of instructions that accompanies your life relationships. The reason is simple—there *is* no instructional manual that covers all of the various situations that you'll encounter as you put together your own relationship!

If you're lucky, you and your partner basically agree on the same set of instructions and the relationship works for many years. If you're not so lucky, you both attempt to construct the relationship in very different ways, and it breaks down. It then either has to be fixed or thrown on the scrap pile as unusable. Can this be avoided? Of course, if you take the time to educate yourself about the product you own and make it a top priority. So it's time to inject a little reality into your life. You and your partner are co-owners of what will be known as a "Life Relationship." As such, you will from this point on be subject to the rules and conditions of said ownership, including the acceptance of what I call "The Relationship Contract."

The Relationship Contract

1. The owner shall be charged with the responsibility of caring for and maintaining the relationship in good working order, by exerting whatever effort is needed to nurture and grow it in positive ways.

2. If a problem arises with the relationship, the owner will make this his or her *top* priority and do whatever is necessary to make it right.

3. The owner will strive to *understand* the reasons for his or her behavior in the relationship, and if these actions are self-destructive, will seek out help.

4. The owner will understand that it's not selfish to verbalize his or her needs in the relationship, and expect the co-owner to at least consider to try to meet these needs.

5. Instead of blaming the co-owner for everything that goes wrong during the course of the relationship, the owner will always search inside to acknowledge his or her part in causing the problems.

You may think that this contract looks like some kind of legalese, but you can't escape the fact that a successful relationship is grounded in these conditions. Simply stated, those who accept these truths will greatly increase their odds at having an intimate, loving, committed relationship for a lifetime. Those who believe that these concepts don't apply to them will most likely run into major relationship problems, and have few skills to solve them.

I'll bet that you didn't say the things in this contract during your marriage vows or when you first decided to exclusively date your partner—after all, it's tough enough to decide that you've found a person with whom to spend a lifetime. But this doesn't change the fact that these five conditions form the basis for your personal happiness! This is the soil from which your relationship will grow and flourish. Ignore these conditions, and the relationship has a good chance of dying—you'll be going nowhere fast. But accept them and you have a realistic chance of developing a wonderful union. The choice seems obvious to me, and I hope that it does to you, also.

I've started out this book with the idea of personal responsibility for one simple reason: If you refuse to see the relationship as yours, you'll probably never do the work necessary to ensure success. You'll continually disregard the ideas in your relationship contract because it's just human nature to not care about things that aren't our own. So make a copy of the contract and post it someplace where you can read it every day. Memorize and try to apply these principles on a daily basis—I'll bet you'll be shocked by how many times you or your partner will break one of the conditions.

The Choices You Make

So let's be crystal clear on this point: It's imperative that you view your personal relationships as an entity that you own. *Every single thing that happens in the course of your relationship is created by you!* Situations that arise could be the direct result of an actual decision, such as:

- You decide who to date or who to marry.

- You decide whether to have children.

- You decide to stay with someone who is good to you, or conversely, you decide to stay with a partner who is mean, disrespectful, or abusive.

- You decide to cheat on your partner.

- You decide to leave a relationship and seek a divorce.

Problems can also occur as a result of indecision or inaction on your part. Remember, you also create experiences by doing nothing or being passive. Here are some examples:

- You don't express your needs in the relationship, so your partner never knows what you really want.

- You don't talk about the problems in your relationship, hoping that the conflicts will just go away.

- You allow your partner to take control and run your life; that is, you act like a child.

- You do nothing to spark any romance and feel as if it's your partner's job to make your sex life great.

- You constantly complain about a terrible relationship, but do nothing to actually change your situation.

Of course, there are many other examples in addition to these. But the end result is the same either way—if you make uninformed decisions or allow bad things to happen, you'll create unhappiness and a difficult relationship experience.

Keep the following equation in mind, and I'll bet that you'll care more about your relationship, because this forces you to acknowledge that the relationship is yours:

The formation of a love relationship with another person = a creation = a possession that you own = a responsibility to care for it each day.

CHAPTER 2

There Is No Set of Relationship Rules That You Must Follow

I MUST ADMIT TO YOU THAT I WAS COMPELLED TO WRITE this book due to the frustration and disappointment I felt about the entire self-help industry. Many people are making millions of dollars capitalizing on relationship failures—it's become a big business.

I don't know who first had the idea to adopt the title of "relationship expert" and dish out some advice, but take a look around you now. Bookstores are jammed with hundreds of titles about relationships—in fact, relationships now have a whole section devoted exclusively to them. It's confusing, even to me, to know which of these authors or books has anything significant to say about the subject.

Yet, we collectively continue to fail in love, as the high rates of divorce and infidelity in our country demonstrate.

It would seem logical to me that if these books were helpful to any great degree, everyone would have the tools to create the relationship of their dreams by now. But sadly, this isn't the case.

I believe that the main problem with these approaches is a continued emphasis on "rules" that must be followed and "secrets" that need to be learned by the reader in order to succeed in love. The only real secret is that those who write and publish these pop psychology books know that most of us like to be told how to behave. They understand that it's comforting for us to feel that there's a cut-and-dried way to manage a love relationship. It's brilliant marketing, but can best be viewed as a one-dimensional and superficial solution to complex life and relationship problems.

The second **Relationship Reality** that you need to accept is this:

There is no set of relationship rules that you must follow. The work to understand your relationship is what's really important.

The authors who are selling you the "Five Easy Secrets" or implying that your relationship can be summed up in a neat little list are doing a great disservice to you. This information doesn't have a real chance of helping your relationship, and these shortcuts won't generally work to save a shaky connection. Emphasizing a quick solution to your problem without helping you first understand your behaviors and motives is a critical mistake. You simply can't solve any conflicts in your relationships without first understanding *why* you're acting in certain ways!

I began to give this reality considerable thought one night when I was watching a TV show that featured the two women who wrote the book *The Rules*. During their media rounds, they claimed that, for a woman to find a man to marry, all she needed to do was follow their instructions, which included such inane pronouncements as "Don't call a man," and "Always play hard to get." They also claimed that a woman should never break their rules or she would meet with failure in finding a man to marry her.

Now, I'm not sure if they had any credentials to tell the public how to manage relationships, or if they even believed in their own set of rules—one of the authors recently announced that she and her husband were divorcing!—but I do know that the concepts were ridiculous, as well as confusing to women who tried to change their personalities to fit into this scheme. Furthermore, their rules didn't even make sense psychologically, because women who hoped to gain relationship power by studying this book may have ended up with the opposite effect—their power was actually taken from them because they were taught to suppress their own free thought and emotions.

The inherent message in a book such as *The Rules* is that there's a right way and a wrong way to handle relationship issues, and that these guidelines apply to everyone—they left no room for a gray zone. But your partnership may be very different from that of your friends or neighbors. Relationships are much too complex to be reduced to a "one-size-fits-all" approach. I always wonder if authors such as *The Rules* ladies actually know going in that their book is going to do very little to actually change anyone's life. Do they put out this material knowing that it has a good chance of selling books, rather than trying to accomplish the goal of helping the reader in a meaningful way? If this is the case, then they're leading you down the road of false promises, and their behavior is downright shameful!

But some of us keep devouring these books, hoping for a magical solution to difficult relationship issues. Have you ever wondered why most of the national women's magazines basically recycle the same articles over and over every month, only changing the cute and trendy titles on the cover? It's pretty simple—because they know that a lot of us want to believe that there's a quick and easy way to "catch" a person, "please" them in bed, and "hold on to" them. There's nothing inherently wrong with these tips, but this approach doesn't force you to put in the thinking and hard work necessary to achieve a deeper, more intimate, and meaningful relationship.

And so we all get fooled from time to time by a catchy slogan, or a self-help guru with an energetic personality and false promises. We buy their book, read it, and then promptly forget all of its information in a few days. Even if some of the material is worthwhile, the guru will be back again soon with the all-new, super-improved relationship potion that of course will need to be bought to replace the old, outdated one. Just be aware that if a book (or series of books) promises you a fast and easy solution to any relationship problem, then that's a book that you should avoid. Save your money and do something nice for your partner—that's a better use of your energy than blindly following someone else's rules for living.

You Can Only Be Yourself

You'll allow for several good things to happen in your relationship if you don't try to follow a set of rules. The first, and most important, outcome of this new way of thinking about your love relationship is: *You're allowed to be yourself!* I know that this concept sounds clichéd, but many people structure their relationships in such a way as to either please their partner or play games to get their own way. In either case, they assume a way of interacting that's not true to their real self. I can't emphasize strongly enough that not only will this behavior ruin your relationship, it will also fragment your own belief systems right down the middle. I know people who have played so many relationship games over the years that they have no idea who they are anymore. They've spent all of their time trying to "play a part," so any sense of a core self is long gone. This is the ultimate, and terrible, price that they must pay for attempting to be what their partner wants, rather than just doing what comes naturally.

I've heard the counter-argument a thousand times: "If someone finds out what I'm really like, then they may not like me. I have to figure out what they want and then become that person."

Unfortunately, the personality that you develop will be based on smoke and mirrors; that is, it will never be representative of the real you. It's a "fake" you, a mirage designed to fool your partner into thinking that you're something you're not. You must believe me when I tell you that this mask will eventually crumble and the relationship will be in real danger of falling apart. I've never met anyone who could consistently follow a bunch of rules that don't feel right internally. Playing games to get someone else to like you will go nowhere fast, because your true self will shine through at some point.

For example, I've spoken to countless men who will intentionally act like jerks to women because they've been told that women don't like nice guys. It starts out like this: A man, who really is a nice guy, instead acts otherwise—the problem with this is that he then gets a woman who's attracted to disrespectful men. He's faked his way into a relationship, which will end quickly when he's unable to maintain the façade. So not only did he lose a relationship, but he was also untrue to himself. It's a lose-lose situation.

If there's any key to having a great relationship, it can only be this certainty: There's someone out there who will like you *for you*. I realize that your search may have seemed futile at times, but the only way to have a true relationship is to allow your partner to fall in love with the real you, flaws and all. Anything short of this is deceitful on your part. Stop listening to the experts who tell you to "be" a certain way. Don't "surrender" to your partner, don't be a "rules" person, and do fight for your right to act naturally in the relationship.

Follow Your Own "Rules"

The attempt to follow a set of predetermined rules will also make your relationship unmanageable for another critical reason: You and your partner will develop rigid and inflexible ways of dealing with disagreements. Of course some conflict is going to happen in your relationships; this is a given. No one can go through life connected to another person and not have frustrating moments. But how you both handle these times will determine whether the relationship will endure or not.

There's another set of rules, not found in any book or magazine, that will affect the quality of your relationship over time—your own set of "internal rules" that just feels right to you. In other words, this represents what you expect of yourself and your partner. Without going into the origin of these internal rules (we will do that in a later chapter), suffice it to say that we all have certain standards that we expect will be met.

But here's where problems can begin. Unfortunately, anyone (and I mean anyone!) with whom you have a love relationship will also have their own rules for living. The equation is simple: Your rules that can't be broken + Your partner's rules that can't be broken = A recipe for potential relationship disaster.

I'm going to ask you to do something that may seem contrary to what you've ever heard before, but bear with me—this idea isn't as crazy as it seems on the surface. Early on in the relationship, you and your partner will agree to throw out your "rule books" and start from scratch. I'm not suggesting that you trash all of your beliefs and values—just that you agree to a spirit of compromise and flexibility in the relationship.

I'll give you an example of how to do this. One of the best things that my wife and I ever did for our relationship was to tackle this exercise. Not only are we clear on our roles, but we rarely argue. We headed off our potential problems at the pass before they had a chance to erode our love for each other.

First of all, we both thought about any rules that couldn't be broken under any circumstances. I wrote mine down, and she did likewise. Obviously, these lists were similar: no cheating, no going to bed angry, no embarrassing the other in public, no spending a lot of money without mutual agreement, no sharing of intimate marital issues with others outside the relationship. One of mine was that Betsy would serve me breakfast in bed each morning and cater to my every need. Just kidding on that one—I wanted to see if you're still paying attention! But you get the point.

Next, we listed the standards that we'd like the other person to meet. This is one step down from the previous ones—not necessary, but desirable behavior. It was amazing how many areas of potential disagreements we had with each other because of ingrained expectations. I learned that I expected a woman to cook and clean up after me, but not to really care how messy the house becomes. I also learned that I expected her to not get angry over "little" things, that is, things *I* deemed unimportant. I've now given up these selfish beliefs.

Our exercise wouldn't have worked, however, if we didn't share a spirit of compromise. So if you're still intent on keeping some relationship rules, then here's another one for you: *You're not always right, and neither is your partner!* Once in a while, you'll have to give in and go along with a plan that feels wrong or just plain dumb to you. But guess what? Your partner then needs to give in sometimes and do what you want, even if they think that it's the craziest idea ever.

Your relationship will run much more smoothly if you both try to adapt to the various challenges that invariably present themselves. Adopting a stance of "I'm right and you're wrong!" not only saps precious positive energy out of the relationship, but it's also not any fun. The unhappiest couples that I've met only know how to work against, instead of with, each other. They both place more value on holding on to antiquated rules, rather than using their energy to develop new compromises, so they argue constantly. Remember, you and your partner are a team—but it's not a competition of winning or losing or seeing who can play the most mind games to get what they want. That team will be destined to lose.

Inherent in the definition of a rule is the belief that something must be done a certain way or it's no good. Let go of this belief right now! There's not a *right* way or a *wrong* way, but a *variety* of ways to handle any relationship interaction. Use your energy to create new solutions, instead of holding on to old solutions that only work for you.

I realize that I started out this chapter by stating that there are no rules. Indulge me for a moment. There actually is one. Here's the true **Golden Rule of Relationships:**

> *If it works for only one of you,*
> *it won't work for your relationship.*

CHAPTER 3

You Need to Take Action!

THE FAIRY TALES THAT WE ALL LEARNED AS CHILDREN always ended with the words " . . . and they lived happily ever after." The prince usually rode off into the sunset with the adoring princess on the back of his horse, and we were left to assume that their lives were now magically transformed. What we didn't hear was that they then had to deal with the kids, the bills, his bad habit of leaving his clothes on the floor, and her tendency to nag constantly! The message that two people can have a great relationship is certainly commendable, but we have no idea how these two individuals actually made it work over the years. The story needs to go on further, but it doesn't, because after all . . . it's only a fairy tale. Life is always grand in a fantasy world, and that's okay, for we all get some hope that maybe *our* relationship will turn out like the ones the characters in those stories had.

But for some of us, things don't turn out quite so nicely. We enter the relationship with high expectations . . . and then the problems begin. The arguments occur day after day, the lines of communication close, the sex dwindles off, and the relationship ends up in serious danger of collapsing. The reality is that, unless something changes, a relationship that begins full of promise will be reduced to one of broken dreams.

Yet most of us do nothing to actively address these issues, nor do we try to tackle the obstacles that stand in the way of our happiness. Intuitively, it would only make sense to acknowledge the problems and then devise a plan to fix them. But this doesn't happen for a lot of us because we continue to live in a fantasy world in which things will just magically get better, without our having to put forth any effort.

I can't tell you how many people over the years have told me that they "hope" that their relationship will improve, in spite of overwhelming evidence to the contrary. Now I'm certainly not saying that hope is a bad thing—if there was no hope in the world, we'd all be in a terrible state. But the fact is that a serious relationship can't survive over the years on "a hope and a prayer." Of course there are wonderful aspects of it, but at its worst, hope is used as an excuse to stay in that nice little fantasy world.

See if any of the following statements are similar to things that you may have said when discussing your relationship:

- "I just hoped that someday he'd start treating me better," from a woman who called my radio show to complain that her husband hadn't bought her a present or recognized her birthday or anniversary for years.

- "I hoped that my wife would stop doing everything her mother ordered," from a man who had no say in family decisions.

- "I hoped that he'd stop going out all night cheating on me," from a client who'd stayed with a man who had been unfaithful to her several times over the years.

Do you feel sorry for any of these people? When I confronted them with the reality that their lives were probably not going to change unless they did something about it themselves, I was met with resistance from every one of them. *Hope is a powerful emotion, but it looks toward the future—it's simply not going to effectively alter a bad situation in your relationship at present.* Change can only occur as a result of decisions you make right now.

I told the wife with the cheating husband that she could hope forever that he would change, but nothing would happen as long as she was accepting the behavior. Hope, for her, was a way to avoid confronting the tough issues in her relationship. She fantasized that her husband was going to be faithful someday, but the chances of this happening were remote. Why? Her fantasy precluded her from demanding fidelity and honesty from her husband. There's simply no reason for any of the spouses described above to change their behaviors, because they can continue to do whatever they want without any real consequences.

The Right Action to Take in Your Relationship

So what should you do? It seems like an overwhelming task to figure out what kind of action will help your relationship and what kind of action will actually make things worse. It's so difficult, in fact, that most people give up in the planning stages and then do nothing at all. But it doesn't have to be this way.

First, be aware that there are actions that lead to positive changes in a relationship—and actions that will lead to negative experiences—for both you and your partner. Therefore, not just any old deed will do—it must be specific and targeted to the behavior that needs to change. Also, some approaches will work well in certain situations but will have no effect on other problems. The key is obviously to figure out the right approach to use with your partner in order to achieve the best results.

Unfortunately, this is often a trial-and-error process. Neither you nor I typically know in advance if our action is right on the money, or if we'll meet with failure. But it doesn't change the basic equation: An *appropriate* action or approach will lead to a positive change in your partner.

There are three basic action steps that should be learned if you want to increase your odds of getting what you want from your partner—and "hope" isn't one of them. The third **Relationship Reality** is this:

> *You must stop living in a fantasy world,*
> *just hoping that things will somehow*
> *change for the better in your relationships.*
> *Change will only occur if you do something.*
> *Take action and set your limits.*

Let's define the actions that lead to productive results.

Step #1: Act Early in the Relationship

One of the basic laws of physics states that the longer an object is in motion, the longer it will tend to stay in that motion. What this means for your relationship is that the longer you allow a partner to act in a certain way, the less likely it is that things will change, even when you finally make a move to put a halt to the behavior. You can't allow your partner to step all over you for years and years and then put your foot down in any meaningful way. Your threats won't be taken seriously. By this time, you've waited too long.

The time to take action, in order to get what you need, is early on in the relationship—that's when you should make it known what the parameters are in your interactions. When things start to get serious with another person, you need to also get serious about what reasonable limits are. Remember this little caveat about human behavior: *Each time that you allow your partner to get away with something that upsets you, the possibility is greater that it will happen again.*

Also note that at some point in the relationship, any attempt by you to change your partner's behavior will be futile if the pattern has been set in place for too long. I don't know what that specific point is for *your* particular relationship, so be proactive and set your limits early. When your partner does something that doesn't sit well with you, make it known that something needs to change. Otherwise, you will have lost any semblance of control and dignity as you continually get stepped on without regard.

Step #2: Realize That Complaining Doesn't Work

Another basic law of physics states that for every action, there is an equal and opposite reaction. For example, let's say that on a weekend day, a wife wants her husband to get off the couch and mow the lawn. She approaches him.

> **Wife:** "Get your butt off that couch and do some work around here for once! I'm so tired of being the only one who does any work around here. You're so lazy!"

> **Husband:** "I'm watching the game! Leave me alone. I'll do it later."

> **Wife:** Lets husband stay on the couch, but mutters, "You never do anything!"

The outcome of this interaction is that now they're both angry, and the yard work still doesn't get done. The husband thinks that the wife is a nag, while she thinks that he doesn't care about her or their property. Consequently, she acts in a hostile fashion, so he withdraws and acts passively. There's absolutely no forward movement.

I can't tell you the number of couples I've seen engage in this cycle of attacking and withdrawing. These people don't understand that angry complaints aren't usually taken seriously by another person—your needs get lost in the translation, and you're branded as a "nag."

Most of the time, it's not what you say that counts, it's how you say it. If you start out your sentences with the words, "You never . . . " or "I always . . . ," then your desire will get lost in the shuffle. An action that has a chance of working will be phrased in *positive* terms first. People simply respond better to positive words than to negative, accusatory words. A smarter approach would have been for the wife in the above example to approach her husband by saying: "I know you want some downtime today, but later, I'd appreciate it if you'd consider mowing the lawn. I can even get things set up for you."

Notice the spirit of cooperation and the acknowledgment of his needs in the above approach—there's no blame, and I'll bet that this tactic has a better chance of getting that lawn mowed. However, you may think that these words sound stiff and unrealistic. If that's the case, at least understand that an angry tone will get you nowhere in a hurry. People tune out complaints and react indifferently or angrily right back.

Stop complaining about what you don't have or what your partner isn't doing—*whining to your friends and family may make you feel better temporarily, but it won't solve your relationship problems!* So make it a challenge to phrase things to your partner in a way that will please *both* of you. If you've ever bought a product impulsively, then you know that sometimes the salesperson "sold" you because they took an empathic, understanding approach, rather than "pushing" something on you. By the same token, chronic complainers are taking an action, but it's just not one that will work consistently. So balance your sentences carefully—with both a positive and a negative—if you need to criticize your partner for any reason. You'll be pleasantly surprised by the favorable results.

Step #3: Draw a Line in the Sand and
Spell Out the Consequences

What if you've tried the positive approach and your partner ignores your request and continues their unacceptable behavior?

Looking back at our examples of people who weren't getting their needs met (from earlier in the chapter), what if the selfish husband is never thoughtful and kind toward his wife? What if the man with the controlling mother-in-law discovers that his wife won't stand up to her mother? What if the woman who constantly was cheated on keeps finding herself in this unfortunate situation? What if your action is met with resistance and your partner disregards your wishes? What will you do then?

It's really sad to see some very decent people put up with a lot of relationship pain due to the fact that any action that they take is met with indifference or anger by their partner. They really try to have a good relationship but simply can't be fulfilled by a disrespectful mate. Yet most of the time, they're too afraid to draw a line in the sand and declare, "That's it! That's all I'm going to take from you!" The lesson here is that your partner will continue to do what they do unless there are consequences for their actions. However, it's up to *you* to define what those ramifications are.

First, you need to define exactly what you will or won't take from a partner. There absolutely must be *dignity* and *respect* toward you from your partner, and *your partner should act in a way that makes you feel good about yourself*. If this is already happening, then don't worry.

But if it isn't, then you need to very specifically define your limits and also decide when you're going to leave the relationship. Then, and here's the hard part, you must communicate these limits! I believe that in any relationship, there's a point when, if your partner continues a pattern of negative behavior toward you, you should leave. So it's only right to give a fair warning.

And now here's the *really* difficult part—you must make good on your promise if your wishes are violated again. Many people are great at threats, but not so good on follow-through. Once you've drawn that line in the sand, you better not keep moving it back. Don't yell, "I won't take it anymore!" if in fact you *will* continue to take it. You're just wasting your words and losing your dignity if you don't take a stand and get what you deserve from your partner.

So what's the moral of the fairy tale that opened up this chapter? By hoping for a positive outcome and fantasizing that your relationship will somehow change for the better, you decrease the chances that anything will happen at all. Changes will only occur from *action* on your part. If you're not getting what you want from the relationship, you must *do something about it!* If your relationship is falling apart, you must *do something to save it!* If you're getting treated badly, you must *do something to stop it!* So get off that ride at Fantasyland and join the other adults who recognize that they need to say what they want and take a stand.

CHAPTER 4

Claim Your Power!

THE FOURTH **RELATIONSHIP REALITY** COULD EASILY BE seen as an extension of the concepts from the last chapter. Maybe you're familiar with the old saying "Fool me once, shame on you. Fool me twice, shame on me."? It may sound like a shopworn phrase, but it's absolutely true. Simply stated:

> *What you allow to happen in your relationship is what you're going to get. Defining what you need and claiming your power is a critical step in maximizing your happiness*

I've often been asked why someone would allow bad things to happen in their relationship. It would only make sense that we all want pleasure and happiness, but some of us seem to have a radar that seeks out partners who inflict pain and disappointment. I'll bet you have a friend (or two) whom you just want to shake and say, "Stop doing that!" or "Why don't you just leave and find somebody else!" It's hard to believe that anyone could stay with a partner who doesn't fulfill their mate's basic needs. But it happens all the time, and it's always sad to watch someone become a victim.

There are a lot of different reasons why you would allow your partner to treat you poorly, but the outcome is always the same: Inherent in the definition of *allowing* is the reality that you give up any control in the relationship, and you end up taking a passive and dependent stance. Your partner's desires and wishes assume a greater importance than your own, and you get treated accordingly. So why would you stand by and let your partner do things that could destroy the relationship? Here are some of the top reasons:

- It's just an extension of how you let *all* people treat you—that is, it's easier for you to be the child in the relationship so that all decisions are made for you.

- You don't like to make waves and will go to any extreme (including sacrificing your self-respect) to avoid arguments or conflicts.

- You adhere to the false hope that, given enough time, your partner will see the light and begin to treat you with respect, even if there have been *years* of disrespect.

- Having *any* kind of relationship, even an unsatisfying one, is better for you than having no relationship at all. It's anxiety-provoking for you to consider the possibility

of being alone, because you desperately
need to be seen as part of a couple.

- Breaking up a relationship would make you
  feel that *you* were a failure, instead of viewing
  the relationship itself as failed.

- You took the vows "for better or for worse"
  and adhere to the belief that *no matter what
  happens,* you'll stay in the relationship and
  just put up with it.

- You and your partner are basically lazy
  and won't put any energy into developing
  positive patterns of interaction. You don't
  go to therapy or seek out help, so you keep
  getting more of the same.

- You've never developed the skills to stand
  on your own and take care of yourself, so
  you find someone else to do it for you.

Do any of these reasons sound familiar to you? They
may, because it's really easy to fall into the trap of allowing
your relationship to slowly fall apart. This relationship
reality hit me one day after I had a series of very frustrating conversations with an acquaintance of mine I'll call
Jane. She'd been married for a couple of years, but the
relationship was going nowhere, so she'd been seeking my
advice. I thought that I was providing very reasonable solutions to the problems she and her husband had, but the
next week, she would come back to me with the same
complaints. Then I realized that I wasn't annoyed with the
content of her marital issues—I was becoming frustrated
with the *way* she described the interactions with her husband.

Jane would start out almost every sentence with the words "He said . . . ," or "He did . . . ," or "He wanted . . . ." Try as I might, I couldn't derail her from describing the relationship in this way. It was as if the whole relationship centered only on him and she was an innocent bystander observing his life. I even tried confronting her and literally saying that I really didn't care what he wanted or was doing! I wanted to know what *she* wanted out of the relationship and how *she* would go about getting it.

But the conversation invariably turned back to him, and it became clear that Jane only existed as an extension of his desires. This probably felt quite good to her husband, since he called all of the shots and did what he wanted, whether she liked it or not. To her, it felt terrible, but she did nothing to change the dynamic.

Finally, I tried a technique that put a dent in her armor. Every single time that Jane would begin another sentence with the word "he," I'd immediately stop her and tell her to rephrase it, beginning with the following: "I chose to allow him to . . ."

Here are a few examples to illustrate this further.

Original Sentence	New Sentence
"He cheated on me."	"I chose to allow him to cheat on me."
"He didn't talk to me."	"I chose to allow him to not talk to me."
"He would rather be with friends."	"I chose to allow him to be with friends."
"He did nothing around the house."	"I chose to allow him to do nothing around the house."

This approach did two things that helped Jane tremendously. First, it forced her to acknowledge that she was actively allowing the relationship to disintegrate, because she'd taken no responsibility for admitting that she was the one who'd given her husband the upper hand in the first place. And second, it forced her to realize that she was *choosing* to tolerate his behavior. If she was ever going to stop being a passive victim, she would have to admit that she was *allowing* him to step on her.

This way of thinking initially seemed foreign to Jane. I expected this, because it's uncomfortable for any of us to realize that we *choose* what will happen in our relationships. But this doesn't change the fact that you'll get whatever you allow your partner to do. For instance, if you demand respect and commitment, that's most likely what you'll get. But if you never say what you want, your partner will probably make the decisions based on what *they* think is right.

So if you now see yourself falling into this pattern, ask what *you're* gaining by allowing your partner's wishes to be more important than your own. A lot of us grow up being told that it's selfish to use the word "I," but that's a fallacy. Using the word "I" makes you accept responsibility for your relationship and helps you define the things you need.

As we learned in the last chapter, *your partner is going to do whatever they do until* you *stop it.* If great things are happening in your relationship, take credit for allowing this to happen. If negative things are happening, you must accept that you're allowing this as well.

It may now be time to firmly say, "I won't tolerate _____ any longer, and I'm going to tell my partner what I would like." *Begin to assert your power!*

Your partner may not always do what you like, but at least you've taken this first step in choosing your destiny. By the way, Jane has now stopped defining her relationship based on what her partner is doing, and has taken charge of getting what *she* wants in life. She's now single, but happy, and I'll bet that her next serious relationship will be much more satisfying because she won't be dominated again.

Don't settle for being in a miserable relationship. *Claim your power and get what you deserve.*

CHAPTER 5

Get Off the Relationship Roller Coaster

I WAS UNEASY. IN FRONT OF ME WERE TWO PEOPLE WHO HAD absolutely no business pledging the rest of their lives to each other, yet as I looked around the church, everyone else seemed to be quite supportive of the bride and groom.

The pastor asked the customary question: "Is there anyone here who knows of a reason why these two people should not be joined in holy matrimony? If so, speak now, or forever hold your peace."

I had the urge to jump out of my seat and scream passionately, "Yes, I know of a great reason! They don't even like each other and can't get along. They'll be divorced in a few years!"

But I sat quietly because I didn't want to make a scene, and also because I've never seen anyone else actually object when this question is posed at weddings. I felt that this marriage was destined to fail, but I wasn't about to ruin a ceremony that had taken months to plan. So I held my peace, ate some good food at the reception, and then went home, absolutely *sure* that this relationship wasn't going to last, or fulfill either person.

But how did I intuitively know that this marriage was a terrible mistake?

Breaking Up and Making Up

It seemed that from the moment they met, Ted and Sheila were constantly arguing about trivial matters. In fact, I actually can't remember a time when they weren't involved in some sort of conflict or relationship drama. Just when things started to calm down, the two of them would fire up another disagreement. They were truly on a roller-coaster ride of emotions that continued to spiral downward.

But somehow their nightmarish ride didn't derail. Just when it looked as if all was lost and the relationship was ready to implode, something interesting always happened, and I'd hear through the grapevine that they were "back together" and flying high. Unfortunately, it was only a matter of time before they would crash and burn again.

The reasons behind their many splits were trivial. They broke up because of a phone call that came too late. They broke up after Ted mentioned a female friend. They broke up over the color of a dress Sheila bought. They got intoxicated at a party, said nasty and hurtful things, and then didn't speak for days. During these breakups, they'd go on other dates so that they could intentionally hurt each other's feelings. Every social event ended with the rest of the guests watching this dynamic duo hurl insults at each other and storm out in separate directions. Everyone, except Ted and Sheila, knew that they were headed for a disastrous denouement.

At one point, I tried to intervene—I expressed my concern to both of them, separately, about the relationship. I wondered aloud if any union could survive this pattern of breaking up and making up, or if perhaps it was a sign that they just weren't meant for each other. My protestations were met with a polite "Thank you, but get out of our life."

And so I did. Ted and Sheila continued on this roller coaster for several more months, argued their way through a fragile engagement, and ended up claiming their "love" for each other in front of their family and friends. But the ride wasn't over: They divorced shortly after their honeymoon.

Ted and Sheila never understood the fifth **Relationship Reality:**

> *If you need to work really hard early in the relationship, then there may be big problems down the road. Get off the relationship roller coaster.*

Love Shouldn't Be Such Hard Work

It's relatively easy from an outsider's point of view to see what went wrong with Ted and Sheila's relationship—but it really doesn't matter what any of us think, since it wasn't our relationship to handle. It was too late to save *them,* but maybe we can all learn something from their experience.

This couple didn't understand one of the fundamental principles that applies to a relationship that will last and flourish: *The early stages of a great relationship shouldn't be filled with conflicts and arguments. If your relationship falls into a pattern of breaking up and making up (also known as The Relationship Roller Coaster), then there's some big trouble ahead.*

The underlying idea we need to discuss here is the concept of *work* in a relationship. I've heard numerous self-help authors state that you must "work at" your relationship to make it . . . work. They claim that for a relationship to grow, there must be a commitment by both partners to tirelessly delve into all their issues.

I can't deny that there will undoubtedly be points in any relationship when compromise, communication, and conflict resolution will be crucial. This is the work in a relationship that may save the whole thing from collapsing. As I brought up when discussing The Relationship Contract, two people must make a commitment to work on their own issues that get in the way, as well as to try to get along on a daily basis. When you work, you expend *energy*, and this is an example of energy well spent.

However, the *early* stages of a love relationship (I'm talking about the first several months—up to the first year or two) should almost be *effortless,* if the relationship is truly right. *You shouldn't have to spend precious energy worrying about whether you'll stay together, or trying to fix things after yet another conflict.*

Consider this for a moment: If you and your partner seem to bring out the worst in each other, even early in the relationship, then perhaps it's just not the right fit. Why force something that causes a lot of pain and heartache, not to mention the time and energy you've spent constantly repairing the relationship? That just doesn't make a whole lot of sense to me—although I know that millions of people hang in there, hoping that things will somehow get better as they board their own personal roller coaster for yet another go.

Why Would You Keep Riding the Relationship Roller Coaster?

It just seems logical that if two individuals engage in a pattern of extreme ups and downs early in their relationship, then they'll recognize the low probability of relationship success between them and move on to other people. But since many don't, we can assume that there must be an extremely powerful force that continues to draw people such as Ted and Sheila together like magnets.

What is it that keeps two otherwise reasonable people coming back for more relationship pain? It must be incredibly strong to override the hurt caused by breakups and bad times. The force is actually grounded in two separate *fallacies of thinking*, which permeate a shaky relationship and cause it to putter along indefinitely.

Fallacy #1: Anything Worth Having Must Be a Struggle

The first fallacy is usually based on the notion in popular culture that the best things in life must be difficult to obtain. A lot of us learned from our parents that good things only happen to people who work hard and earn their rewards. I've heard the saying "Nothing in life is free!" many times throughout my life.

Yet this way of thinking may actually be counter-productive to a great love relationship. This is because we naturally equate success with the amount of work expended in the process, so more work must equal more success. However, in the early stages of a relationship, this concept simply doesn't hold up. A relationship that has a chance of surviving follows the *opposite equation:*

Fewer relationship problems = less energy expended on conflicts and differences = a more successful relationship.

So before you think that significant disagreements and differences will make your relationship stronger, consider that my equation may have some merit. There are some people in this world whom you will simply never connect with on a deeper level. Holding on to a relationship that suffers from constant arguing and effort is not only foolish, but also squanders valuable energy. Use your strength to find the right partner, rather than wasting it by struggling to make an unhealthy relationship work for you.

Fallacy #2: We Can *Make* It Work!

Recently I was talking to Dan, a friend of mine who was becoming seriously involved with a woman he'd met just a few months before. Within that time span, they'd broken off the relationship several times and really didn't even seem to like each other.

Yet when I queried Dan on the likelihood that he and his girlfriend would stay together, he proudly stated,

"We can make it work—I know we can! We're both intelligent people. The relationship will get better."

I tried to point out that believing that they would somehow overcome a destructive pattern of conflicts so early in their relationship process was the height of naive and grandiose thinking, but he would have none of it. He remained convinced that they were like Romeo and Juliet— star-crossed lovers who would find a way to rise above insurmountable odds.

The problem with Dan's approach was that he was living out a relationship *fantasy*, instead of assessing the *reality* of the situation. He was simply overconfident in his ability to fix his malfunctioning relationship. He didn't realize that some love unions are just not meant to be. Dan overlooked the serious differences in life philosophies between him and his girlfriend. He also ignored the warning signs (the breaking up and making up) that foreshadowed the end of the relationship. He tried to make it work with the wrong person—an action that would surely only lead to wasted time. Unfortunately, it took him over a year to finally get it, when he should have seen the trouble coming much earlier.

So what's the lesson here? *If you believe that you possess some special talent to save a relationship mired in anger and conflict, then be very careful.* Maybe you'll get lucky as both of you mature in the relationship—but maybe you won't. At least open your eyes to the possibility that the break-up/make-up cycle will *not* lead to a stable, happy love relationship.

The Thrill of Riding the Roller Coaster

If you've ever ridden a real roller coaster at an amusement park, you'll know exactly what I'm talking about here. There's something addictive about this experience that keeps a lot of people coming back for more. It has to do with the exhilaration and excitement you feel when you climb those steep inclines and plummet down the other side. That shot of adrenaline through your body feels so good that, even if you're scared, you crave the experience again and again.

Some relationships work in the same way. There's an upside to the make-up process that drives us to continue the relationship. When we make up, there's usually some great sex, an exchange of sweet nothings, cards or love letters being sent, and a chance to relive the honeymoon all over again. We get treated (at least for a little while) the way we deserve to be treated, and it feels great! Making up proves to us that we're desirable and lovable—it validates all of our deepest relationship insecurities. We subsequently delude ourselves into believing that *"if my partner desperately wants me again, it must mean that I'm worthwhile as an individual."*

Of course you're a special and worthwhile person, *but also consider that you could just be swept away by the reconnection, while missing the point of why the relationship broke up in the first place.* I know of many couples who made up and their relationship is still going strong—but first they tried to figure out *why* they got to the point of needing to make up. They looked at their relationship problems in an objective fashion, instead of getting caught up in the emotional whirlwind of the flowers and the pleas for "one last chance."

🐚 🐚 🐚

I understand that any good relationship that grows over time takes a certain amount of work and introspection—I'm certainly not arguing this fact. If you're with your partner for years and years, there will be differences that need to be settled, which require time and energy. My point is simply that the formative or early stages of that relationship should *not* be filled with arguments and conflicts that cause breakups. It's tempting to want that special feeling that you get when your partner begs for forgiveness. But when you hear yourself saying, "I'm so happy we're back together!" ask this question also: *Should I be?*

CHAPTER 6

Say What You Need to Say

WOULDN'T IT BE NICE IF OUR PARTNERS COULD JUST instinctively know what we wanted and then immediately meet all of our desires? In a world where we get pampered and treated as if all of life revolved around us, why should we waste our time *asking* for anything? Imagine this: You're like one of those ancient kings who lounges about while an attentive staff caters to your every whim. You snap your fingers and they just immediately intuit your needs.

Unfortunately, you and I aren't royalty. And chances are, unless you've married a psychic, *your partner can't read your mind!* Even celebrities, with their entourages of people paid to serve them, still have to do things the hard way when it comes to their relationships.

That's right—good old-fashioned communication is absolutely required if you're to have any kind of intimate, long-term relationship. It's not fun, and it's often time-consuming, but there's no way around this sixth **Relationship Reality:**

> *If you need something, the only way to get it will be to tell your partner. No one can read your mind.*

Learn to Speak Up

I've been asked many times to define the number-one reason why people finally get to the point of separation and divorce. Naturally, there are different reasons for different couples, but it usually comes down to a variation on the same theme: At some point in time, you or your partner stop verbalizing your wants and needs. The process is simple: When people have expectations (on any level) that are unmet, they'll most likely become very unhappy. They'll pout, withdraw, get angry, and generally act in unpleasant ways that aren't part of their normal character.

But why would our partner not meet our expectations? Is it because they've hatched some secret evil plan to make us miserable? Do they like to see us upset and frustrated every day? In most instances, this is far from the case. The truth is: *We usually don't get our expectations met because our partner just doesn't know what we want.*

Read that sentence again, because this may be one of the most important concepts that I'll offer in the entire book. You won't get the things you desire if you don't find a way to express these wishes to your partner. The way, in and of itself, doesn't matter—tell them, write them a letter, show them, go to the top of the nearest building and shout it with a mega-phone—I don't care how you do it, but *express your needs!*

I'm making a big assumption here—that you recognize the expectations you bring to a relationship, because in order to articulate your needs, you must know what they are first. Yet when I've asked couples over the years what it is that they specifically need, the answer is usually along the lines of, "I just want to be happy." This response just isn't sufficient. If you only have a vague idea of what you want, then you'll only get vague things in return. I really don't have a clue what "happy" means to you, and your partner probably doesn't intuitively know that either. So, *to get specific things, you must ask for specific things, no matter how small or trivial these things seem.*

Let's illustrate this point with an example that follows a typical chain of events: John and Laura don't know what the other expects in their relationship. John was raised in a household where his mother did all of the chores for the family. She cooked and cleaned, while John focused on his schoolwork. If John *did* make a mess—such as tossing his clothes around or not cleaning up after him-self—it was no big deal. His mother was always right behind him, cheerfully taking care of his life.

Laura, on the other hand, was raised with the notion that every family member pulled their weight, and she was given a list of duties that she was expected to complete each day. Consequently, she now lives to organize, and a messy house just drives her crazy. Yet, for some reason, she lets John slide on his responsibilities, so he does what he's familiar with—he throws his clothes on the floor, doesn't take out the garbage, and never washes the dishes after dinner. There are many reasons why Laura doesn't express what she needs from John (which I'll get to later), but the end result is that these little irritations start to build up. Laura is upset, but she thinks that maybe she shouldn't turn John's annoying little habits into a huge argument.

So a lot of time passes, with Laura's frustration mounting, and there's no resolution in sight. She begins to feel that if John *really* cared about her, he'd recognize this lack of respect and just change on his own. She finally comes to the conclusion that John must not really love her, since he continues to exhibit behavior that she deems intolerable.

See if the following conversation sounds familiar to you.

Laura: "I'm so tired of your not doing anything around here! I'm not your mother. Pick up your stuff!"

John: "Wait a minute. Why are you getting mad all of a sudden?"

Laura: "Because you're a slob! I'm not going to clean up after you anymore."

John: (now angry) "Hey, it's the least you could do for me! I work all day long to support this family, and all I get in return is you yelling at me."

Laura: "All I'm asking is that you make an effort."

John: (defensively) "Well, it never bothered you before." (He storms out of the room.)

A few hours later, John can't understand it when he wants to get romantic with Laura and she rejects his advances. Another argument ensues, and they don't even speak to each other the next day.

So who do you think is most at fault here? If you're like most people I've had analyze this interaction, you'll probably blame John more than Laura. You probably think that he's acting like a jerk (you're right), and that he should start to respect his wife by modifying his messy behavior. It may surprise you to learn, however, that I tend to blame Laura. How could this be? After all, a number of mistakes were made by each of them during this heated exchange.

> *Mistake #1*—Laura's approach: blaming and ordering. This will only serve to make John defensive and angry. Implying that John is still a child won't serve to express her needs in a way that he'll hear.

> *Mistake #2*—John's attempt to distract Laura from his flaws. By referring to how hard he works, he essentially negates her feelings and sends the conversation in an unrelated direction.

But the biggest mistake of all actually occurred long *before* their angry interaction. When John says, "Well, it never bothered you before," he's right, as far as he'd been led to believe. This is a reasonable assumption on his part, although you may argue that he should have known that his habits would bother any normal person. Nevertheless, Laura must shoulder the blame *for not ever saying what she needed and expected* from John in the relationship. John was simply doing what he's always done (right or wrong)—it was up to Laura to communicate her displeasure, and she failed to do so. She let a bad pattern establish over the course of the relationship, and then expected a sudden end to her husband's sloppiness. Like most things in life, the longer you let someone get away with something, the harder it will be to quickly change the dynamic.

So you must get over the feeling that it's selfish to communicate your expectations. In fact, one of the characteristics of someone who's grown up is the ability to respectfully ask their partner to consider their needs. Children have parents to do things for them, so they aren't forced to express their requirements. But you're not a child anymore, and you can't expect your partner to magically know what you want. *Adults define the things that will make them happy, and then develop a plan to achieve the desired result.* At the very least, it's naive to believe that your partner will automatically satisfy all of your wishes without some direction from you.

The Path to Getting Your Needs Met

So how do you begin this process? I understand that it's a daunting task to acknowledge your needs in a relationship and then to actually communicate them to another person. Usually the excuse for this procrastination is something like: "He won't do it anyway, so what's the use of asking?" I counter this statement with the challenge that you have absolutely *no* chance of getting what you want if you don't ask for it. If you're not being fulfilled emotionally or sexually by your partner, then it's time to take action. What is truly the worst thing that could happen if you ask your partner to do some specific thing? With few exceptions, all they can do is say no, and then you know where things stand.

So let's diagram a simple algorithm that defines the *correct path to getting needs met*:

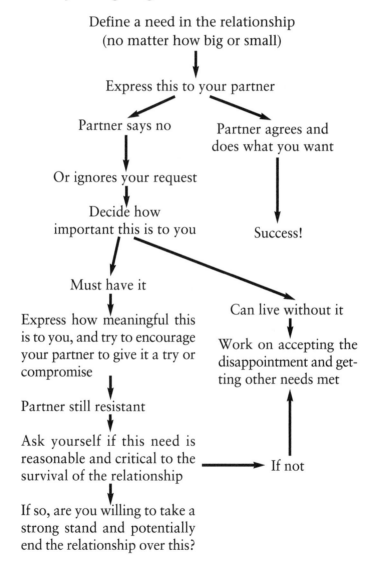

Define a need in the relationship
(no matter how big or small)

Express this to your partner

Partner says no   Partner agrees and
                                   does what you want

Or ignores your request

Decide how
important this is to you   Success!

Must have it

                                   Can live without it
Express how meaningful this
is to you, and try to encourage   Work on accepting the
your partner to give it a try or   disappointment and get-
compromise   ting other needs met

Partner still resistant

Ask yourself if this need is
reasonable and critical to the
survival of the relationship ————▶ If not

If so, are you willing to take a
strong stand and potentially
end the relationship over this?

You should be getting the message that at some point you'll have to decide whether to draw that line in the sand and demand that your partner do certain things in order to keep the relationship viable. Neither I nor anyone else can define this for you. My personal opinion of what you need for your own relationship isn't going to help you from day to day. The only thing that counts is what *you* define as necessary, and then go about telling your partner what that is.

For instance, a woman I know named Kim decided that she needed her husband to tell her what time he would return home from work each day. She also expected them to eat dinner together every night, since she felt that this was an important time for her to talk to her husband. She told her husband her needs, he agreed, and the relationship flourished. I asked her once what she would have done if he had refused to respect her wishes. Her reply was that this expectation was so crucial to her that she would have considered ending the relationship and finding someone who *would* acquiesce to her needs.

The same challenge applies to you: *Start defining the things you absolutely need from your partner in several critical areas.* For most people, this centers on issues of commitment and fidelity, sexual relations, family dynamics, children, and finances.

So indulge me as I present three principles that you might follow in this regard:

Principle #1—The Time to Make Your Needs Known Isn't During the Heat of Battle

Many people make this error—they let their grievances pile up over time, and then they explode one day over some unrelated matter. The time to talk about your expectations in the relationship is *before* the problem arises. For instance, if you really want children, you should find out if your partner feels the same way before you get married and then spend your life childless. If you won't tolerate infidelity, then you'd better make this clear early on—before you find out one day that there's been an affair going on behind your back. If you desire a certain amount of romance and sexuality in your relationship, or if you want your partner to do something specific for you, then *ask for it.* Don't go to bed silently fuming every night.

Principle #2—Be Aware That Things That Are Extremely Important to You May Not Seem So Important to Your Partner

I usually forget to turn off the lights when I leave a room, and I don't think it's a big deal, but this bad habit grates on my wife, so she let me know about it. I still don't think it should be that important in the grand scheme of things, but out of respect for her, I now attempt to hit that "off" switch. Would we end up divorced if I didn't do this? Probably not, but I try to honor her request nonetheless. By the same token, your partner should try to respect your needs, and you should try to consider theirs. No matter how crazy the requirement may seem (unless it's destructive or hurtful), mull it over and then try to engage in some sort of dialogue. Neither of you will always get what you want, so be prepared for some negotiation, and don't take a *no* as a personal rejection.

Principle #3—Realize That It Takes a Lot of Guts to Ask for Something, Since the Possibility of Rejection Always Looms Large

But remember this: Determining your compatibility with a potential lifemate depends on deciding whether you have common expectations and needs for the relationship. This is no time to be afraid of what the other person may think of you. Holding in your desires because you're scared of being rejected will only hurt the relationship in the long run. And years of giving in to all of your partner's needs, while forsaking your own, will only lead to a deep sense of resentment. If your partner does something that you don't like, summon up the courage to tell them the very first time. If it becomes a pattern, then when you finally do speak up, your words will ring hollow, because you've "taken it" for so long.

So start making these phrases a regular part of your vocabulary, beginning right now: "I would really like it if you/we could _____ ," or "I really need you to _____." You can never hope to have a deep, intimate relationship for a lifetime unless you take those first few baby steps.

CHAPTER 7

Timing Is Everything

Y OU'VE TAKEN A BIG STEP FORWARD AND HAVE DEFINED a need. Now you need a relationship—but not just any relationship—you're on the lookout for a lifetime partner. Maybe you're tired of the dating scene, or perhaps you think it's just time to settle down. But whatever the reason, your biological clock says that it's time to find "Mr. (or Ms.) Right."

Yet isn't it ironic that at the precise moment you're ready for a commitment, you usually have the most trouble finding that special person? A sense of desperation can set in—leaving you quite unappealing to potential mates.

I personally know that this is true, because after several unsuccessful dating experiences, I started to feel despondent. I wanted to keep going out on dates, but the pain of not finding someone right for me was too consuming. And then it happened—at a time when I wasn't even looking, I met my future wife. It was lucky for me that I hadn't become so bitter that I closed myself off to a new relationship. But I did have to learn the hard way, so I understood the seventh **Relationship Reality** all too well:

> *The right timing is a crucial factor in determining whether a particular relationship will progress. Just because you're ready doesn't mean that a potential partner will move at the same speed.*

The painful actuality is that even if you've met the right person, the timing could be off. If this is the case, a relationship with that "perfect" person really has little chance of going in a positive direction.

Why is timing so crucial in determining whether or not you'll find true happiness with your partner? Because *if you and your partner want different things in important areas of the relationship at different times, there will always be unmet expectations and disappointments.* Unless these feelings are processed in a mature way, anger and resentment usually follow, and two people who may really love each other will then go careening toward relationship disaster. I've treated a number of couples in my practice and on the radio whose relationships met an untimely end simply because of different goals at different times. Most of these people truly loved each other, but due to the fact that they'd reached an impasse, they didn't end up staying together in the long run. This is sad, but it happens more often than you might think. In fact, it's probably even happened to you with someone you felt was "the one" . . . before everything fell apart.

The Big Decisions

Special attention needs to be paid to two critical decision points for most couples—when to get married (committed) and when to start a family. These are the two "biggies" for any couple—straight or gay.

I believe that most people in the world *do* want to bond with another human being. Life would be pretty lonely without a shoulder to cry on, or without a smiling face to share your joy. We all want to feel loved and needed, and we do have a biological instinct to pair off for life. But the hard lesson is this—people move at different speeds in this process, and there's not much you can do to change someone else's pace. In fact, the attempt to force your partner into your gear is generally counterproductive.

I fielded a call from Marian, who complained that she'd been engaged for six years, and now she really wanted to marry her fiancé, Greg. He, however, had other ideas, and made dozens of weak excuses to postpone the wedding. They were at a standoff, as Marian wanted to take the relationship further, and Greg wanted to maintain the status quo. They rarely slept together anymore, and they constantly argued about other things unrelated to the real problem. He finally told her that he would let her know when he was ready . . . that had been three years prior. She wanted to know if she should now "force" him to marry her or just call the whole thing off.

I recounted the positive and negative ways that this approach could play out. If it went positively, they would finally get married. This is what Marian desperately wanted, as she hoped Greg would subsequently settle nicely into married life. But then I showed her the negative side to this coin—people who are "forced" to do something before they're ready will many times act out and ultimately ruin the relationship. The bottom line was that Marian was taking a huge chance either way—by calling it off, she risked losing the love of her life; but by giving Greg the ultimatum, she'd be forcing something unnatural to happen.

However, I offered Marian a third choice, one that didn't seem so obvious: Why not define a reasonable amount of time in which she and Greg would both agree to work toward marriage? This could include couples counseling, with discussions about Greg's fears of a lifetime commitment and Marian's need to formalize their relationship with a marriage ceremony. If he was unwilling to take the next step after that time, it would be logical for her to conclude that they were on two very different wavelengths. Her option would then be to decide how important marriage was to her. If Marian was absolutely adamant about it, then she'd have to start the process of breaking up with Greg and moving on.

Do You and Your Partner Have the Same Timetable?

You're probably getting the picture that wrong timing between two people can lead to considerable anguish. This is one of the most frustrating aspects of a relationship for me to write about, because there are no cut-and-dried answers. The exact time when you decide to exclusively date one other person, get married, have children, or decrease your working hours to spend more time at home—is crucial. Never underestimate the difficulty you or your partner will have in reaching these decisions.

I can say one thing with some certainty, though: A good rule of thumb is that if your relationship seems like a lot of work—that is, if getting your partner to agree to move forward is like pulling teeth—then you've got trouble ahead. Relationships that survive have this in common: *The partners don't have to constantly argue about when to reach milestones.* Neither one has to wait for years until life-changing issues (marriage, children, careers, and so on) are settled. In fact, I think it's a mistake to let things go on for an extended period of time. You need to find out fairly early on what your partner's attitudes are regarding these central issues—*especially* about commitment and children. If their opinions differ radically from yours, know that a lack of synchronistic timing may end the relationship.

This is one of the most difficult realities for any of us to accept, especially if your partner seems like the right person in all other ways. *But just because you're ready for a relationship doesn't mean that your partner is also ready.* For instance, you may want to start a family when you reach a certain age, but this doesn't mean that your partner will go along with it. You or your partner may not be ready to make sacrifices on the career front in order to put the time into developing a serious relationship. You may meet someone just when they're rebounding off of a long relationship, and mistakenly expect that they'll quickly want to be with you on an intimate level, when they're far from ready for that.

I hope that you'll have a bit of luck on your side and you'll meet the right person at exactly the right time. But listen closely to what your partner says to you. If you hear, "I'm not ready to commit," or "I'm not ready to start a family," *believe it.* Don't take it for granted that these attitudes will change.

One of the saddest stories that I've seen in a long time played out on a television talk show recently. When Sara was in her late 20s and David was in his mid-50s, they got married. Both admitted that David had been very clear up front that he didn't want children at any time. But Sara thought that, when enough time had passed, he'd change his mind. Now, years later, they were on the verge of breaking up because Sara, now in her 30s, insisted it was time to have a family. David resisted, accurately pointing out that she knew all along that he had no intention of having children. It was heartbreaking to watch two decent people enter a lose-lose situation, for in order for the relationship to work, one of them would have to make a huge sacrifice. At this point, there's not much advice that will resolve an issue such as this or make Sara and David feel any better. Her mistake was made long before by not understanding the risk she would take by continuing the relationship.

So minimize your chance of a future broken heart by *listening* to the statements made by your partner. Then, don't naively assume that they "really don't mean it." Understand that it's very risky to stay with someone who's giving clear signals that they want to keep seeing other people or don't want a family. If you're a gambler, it could possibly be worth the wait at some point . . . but you could also lose many years without ever getting what you really want.

Let's sum up the last two chapters in this way: *You must actively define the things that you need and are important to you, and then go about finding someone else who shares these same goals at the same time.* Otherwise, you'll be forever subject to your partner's timetable in life. Don't live out your relationships so that you'll look back and feel cheated out of the things you really desired.

Remember this equation: *Right person + right timing = right relationship.* Anything less will lead to disappointment.

CHAPTER 8

Having Children
Will Not Save a Relationship

EFORE WE GO ANY FURTHER, I'D LIKE TO PREFACE THIS chapter with the following statement: Having a family is an enriching experience for countless couples, as children usually make their lives and relationships better. I say this first so I won't be accused of only looking at the negative aspects of raising kids. I suspect that by the end of this chapter, many people will be angry with me and disagree with my views, but, nevertheless, let's press on with a reality that can't be understated.

The eighth **Relationship Reality** is this:

> *A relationship with a shaky foundation will probably not get better with the addition of children.*

You may think that this sounds like a harsh, uncaring statement, but it's true. In the last 20 years or so, we've been faced with unprecedented numbers of unwed mothers and pregnant teens. More and more children are growing up in broken homes, victims of parents who couldn't make their marriages work. And in quite a few situations, after the baby is born, the father immediately ends the relationship with the mother and essentially vanishes.

Of course, there are thousands of women and men who choose to have a child (by pregnancy or adoption) without a relationship. This discussion is not directed at them, because most of these people do a fabulous job of raising their children. Please understand that I'm not criticizing single parents, nor am I trying to make the political argument that only an intact nuclear family must be in place to ensure the health and happiness of the children. I understand this conservative view, but I also realize that single parents make great sacrifices for their kids and, more often than not, produce well-adjusted, happy children.

This reality is directed at anyone who thinks that having a child will automatically strengthen a relationship. I've heard countless women (and some men) say that they secretly hoped that by having a child their already shaky relationship would improve. The fantasy is always the same—the person's partner will love them more and want to stay around because they created a child together. These individuals are often disillusioned and know that things are going badly, but they've been told that children always create a deeper bond between parents.

What these people don't understand (or underestimate) is that raising a child is also an extremely stressful experience—I've never heard otherwise from *any* parent. This doesn't imply that there aren't going to be good times, but it does mean that a massive life adjustment will take place. A child causes parents to change their lives and rearrange priorities—by necessity, things will drastically change after a baby is brought into the picture.

Parental Guidance

When any of us are faced with a dramatic, life-altering event—such as the addition of a child to our household—there's a typical chain of events that occurs. After the newness wears off, we're then left to deal with the day-to-day reality of the situation. We will also be facing several decision points and questions that must be answered. In this case, the questions include: Who will assume the care of the children? Who gets up in the middle of the night to feed and comfort them? Who keeps working and who stays home? Will we hire a nanny or utilize day care? Who makes the rules and doles out the punishment? The list could go on and on, but be aware that these are just a few of the important questions a couple needs to ask themselves.

I wish that there was some sort of national mandate that forced couples who want children to at least take a *course* on how to parent! My idea isn't to shove some ideology or theory at potential parents, but to merely give them the chance to explore their concerns in the presence of a trained moderator or counselor. Unfortunately, this type of pre-parenting counseling rarely occurs, so we're left to struggle with these issues by using whatever handling skills we've developed.

And that's when the problems arise. Being in charge of a totally dependent child is a responsibility that some people just can't handle. It's frightening and overwhelming, and you can bet that some of the parents' worst character traits will surface. I've seen many couples use old, maladaptive coping techniques at this time because they're anxious and have little experience to fall back on. Instead of coming together as a team, they start to come apart, and the cracks in their relationship begin to widen. Remember: *Most relationship weaknesses will only be magnified as a couple deals with the pressures of parenting.*

This is just straightforward psychological theory—that when the pressure's on, we'll revert back to ways of coping that we're familiar with. In this case, sometimes the couple will pull together and create an experience that does lead to an amazing bond between them. Other times, though, the child will only represent a new stressor that can't be managed, leading to a cycle of anger, blame, and resentment.

Starting a family can expose new relationship weaknesses that must be met head-on—but previously unresolved relationship issues will crop up as well. In other words, if you have a relationship problem before you have children, it's probably not going to get better—in fact, it may get worse. It may be easy to blame the child, but it's simply not their fault. *You're* the one who made the decision to bring them into the world, so you're the one who has to take care of the relationship with your partner. What this means is that you'd better be sure that your relationship is on pretty solid ground *before* you make the decision to start a family. In a practical sense, this translates into several *guidelines* that are wise to adhere to:

- *Both* partners must agree that they want children, and also agree on the timing of this event. Unexpected pregnancies do occur, but steps should be taken to avoid them. If you or your partner gets "talked into" having a child, the stage is set for future resentment.

- You and your partner should be committed to the relationship for the long haul—trying to have a child while dating or breaking up is a very bad idea.

- Be prepared to face some entirely new relationship problems, and insist that your partner be open to discussing how the child might change your lives.

- Before the birth, you and your partner need to discuss your views on how a child should be raised, and try to share some of the things you both experienced as children. Look at the positive things your own parents did when raising you, as well as some of the not-so-admirable things.

- If neither of you is ready for a family, don't just hope that the woman won't get pregnant—practice responsible family planning. Ask yourself *every* time that you have sex: "Are we ready to potentially bring a child into the world?"

I implore you to discuss these issues before you start a family. This is a complex and difficult subject to tackle, but please consider one very important concept: Nine times out of ten, the process does *not* go in this way: *Weak relationship + birth of child = strong relationship.*

Usually, the process is more like this: *Relationship on unsteady ground + birth of child = relationship that's in great danger of falling apart,* unless the couple makes a firm commitment to deal with their relationship problems.

So if you're in a relationship filled with anger, unhappiness, or indecision about the future, do yourself a favor and hold off on having children. This is not just fair to you and your partner, but more important, it's the right thing to do for your future child, who doesn't deserve to grow up in a home where the adults can't get along. Your kids can only develop based on what they see, and bringing children into an already dysfunctional relationship isn't doing anyone any favors. Not only that, but using a child as a pawn in an attempt to create a better relationship with your partner is just plain wrong. This is naive thinking, which could lead to negative consequences for your relationship and your children.

So, deal with your relationship baggage first, before you make your kids carry it. It's just too heavy for them, and will likely weigh them down for the rest of their lives. That's an unfair burden for anyone to have to shoulder—least of all, an innocent child.

CHAPTER 9

You Can't Always Get
What You Want

THERE'S BEEN A FUNDAMENTAL CHANGE IN OUR COLLECTIVE psyche over the past couple of decades. We, as a society, have evolved into thinking differently about ourselves and the world. I know that every past generation claims not to "get" the new trends and fashions, but this change is more insidious, and certainly more threatening to the fabric of healthy relationships.

We're the *"me"* generation, thrust into a much faster-paced world, where products and services are just a click away. We expect immediate results, and we usually get them—but when we don't, our levels of entitlement and anger reach epic proportions. With new technology comes the feeling that we *should* have whatever we want, instead of the reality that most things in life are earned as a privilege.

So if we aren't satisfied, we sue 'em, or blame somebody else, or throw a fit that "our needs aren't being met." This is simply the way that a lot of us cope now.

The attitude is this: We want it *now*, made to order, just how we like it! Better yet, give it to us ten minutes ago, or else you've been a major disappointment. Unfortunately, this doesn't just apply to our jobs and business anymore—this feeling permeates many personal and romantic relationships. We come to expect a lot more than our partner is able to give, and when things don't automatically fall into place, we become children, pouting and digging our heels in. We don't want to do the work that might actually *solve* the problems. Yet this approach contradicts common sense and basic decency. And so, as a voice of reason, I state the ninth **Relationship Reality**:

> *You can't always get what you want in any relationship. Great relationships happen as a result of both partners developing selfless attitudes.*

Nobody's Perfect—Not Even You!

I know what you're thinking now. You don't see yourself as a greedy, self-centered child who throws temper tantrums when things don't go your way. You, like most people, probably view yourself as a reasonable individual with good intentions. Maybe your partner is someone who takes more from you than they give back—you may feel that you've given a tremendous amount and made great sacrifices, without receiving much appreciation for your efforts in the relationship. You've been keeping score, and it's about time to reap the rewards of praise and attention that you so richly deserve.

The problem is that nothing that anyone's done has ever been quite *enough*. For a variety of reasons, your partners have always fallen just a bit short of your expectations, and then you feel a deep sense of disappointment. Perhaps you've looked at other couples and have thought that they must really know the secret to happiness and are doing something that you're not. You've been in search of the "perfect" relationship—one in which both you and your partner are always on the same wavelength and want identical things from life.

This kind of relationship would be great . . . if it were possible. But it's not, and the quicker you accept this fact, the better off you'll be. A relationship can't be all things to you all of the time. It's virtually impossible for your partner to satisfy all of your desires; moreover, it's not even their job to do so. Keep in mind that *your partner exists in the relationship to enhance your life, rather than to make up for your own deficiencies, which you haven't taken care of on your own.*

Adapting to this way of thinking could literally be enough to save a broken partnership, or free you to create a new one that turns out better than before. How do I know this? Because for years I lived through the pain of relationships that went sour due to my belief that all I needed in order to feel good about myself was to be with someone. I wanted it *all* from a partner, and when she fell short of my heightened expectations or didn't please me, the relationship ended. What I didn't realize was that my girlfriends were just doing the best they could, but each partnership was a setup for failure from the start. For instance, I remember complaining to friends that "she just wasn't doing enough," or finding some flaw that always prevented the relationship from going to the next level. I distinctly recall that when a disagreement arose, I would characteristically devalue the relationship if my partner wouldn't come around to my way of thinking. My critical mistake was to believe that the relationship should serve to make me happier, when the reality was just the opposite.

The difficult lesson to be learned was this: *I was not able to maintain a life relationship until I was happy with myself first.* I'm sure that a lot of my past partners could sense this quality about me—I wanted something "from" them on my terms, instead of wanting to just "be" with them. It went both ways, too—sometimes they'd tire of me, while other times, I would be the one to find something wrong and I'd move on.

What finally changed this painful dynamic for me was to step back from having relationships. In what would turn out to be one of the best moves of my life, I went on a dating sabbatical and did some thinking about why no one had ever measured up to my ideal. The key was my decision to make this completely open-ended, as I would only start to seek out a new relationship when it felt right to me again.

Then something wonderful happened: Without knowing it at the time, I started to subtly shift my way of interacting with people. I completely removed the self-imposed pressure to "get" something out of the interaction—be it a business card, a phone number, or a date. I also removed one other overwhelming need—the desire to get others (especially potential dates) to like me. It's not that I went out of my way to appear rude to new acquaintances, but I simply didn't care whether the relationship ever went any further. I tried to live in the moment, to accept the interaction at face value, and to simply connect with people. If it led to a friendship, fine—if not, I tried not to dwell on it.

Without being consciously aware of this change in my personality, I began the process of going from a *selfish* view of relationships to a *selfless* view. It was only after this transformation had occurred that I was able to have a realistic chance of creating a lifelong relationship, for I then met the woman who would become my wife. But this isn't just about me—this transformation has to happen for you, too, if you're ever going to achieve a relationship for a lifetime.

Selfish vs. Selfless

So let's spend a few moments discussing what it means to structure your relationship in a selfless way. The great majority of people who fail at relationships have never thought about this concept, as they selfishly adhere to the belief that their partner is on this planet to fill up the emptiness they feel inside.

The concept of *selfishness* is basically defined as a need to be the center of attention, only caring what happens to oneself in a relationship. Here are a few examples of what a *selfish* partner does:

1. They have great difficulty accepting the reality that their partner will have some different values and beliefs that are just as valuable and productive as their own.

2. They expect things to be done their way, or no way at all. The selfish partner can't tolerate independent action and thinking from their partner.

3. They find a flaw in their partner and use this as an excuse for a lack of intimacy or as a convenient way to end the relationship. The selfish partner will seize on one quality, instead of the whole person, as vital to the success of the relationship—for instance, they'll leave a partner because of looks or a host of other superficial or material reasons.

4. They idealize their partner as someone who has the job of making them "happy," forcing the partner into the role of caretaker and decision maker—whether they desire this role or not.

5. Most important, they can't tolerate ambiguity in a relationship. The selfish partner will hold to the foolish belief that every relationship problem that arises must be solved in a black-or-white fashion. They must have an answer to every disagreement with their partner in order to reduce their own internal anxieties, and they will rarely compromise their position.

Do any of these qualities sound familiar to you, either about yourself or your partner? Of course, we're *all* selfish at times in our relationships, without even knowing it. Usually this doesn't ruin the entire thing, but being selfish shouldn't detract from the need for all of us to become more selfless in our lives.

The people that I know who have created fabulous relationships all understand the *selfless* approach. (Notice that each one of these qualities is the antithesis of the selfish attitudes listed above.)

1. They are able to see their mate as an independent entity, not merely as a puppet that must agree with certain specified values and beliefs. A selfless person doesn't fight the inevitable differences in backgrounds and needs that are a part of any relationship. Instead, they realize that there's no way around these things, and accept that their partner has a right to place importance on issues that may seem initially trivial. A selfless person is open to dialogue, rather than shutting down difficult discussions.

2. They will sometimes let their mate have their way, even if it means that they have to give up control and let the chips fall where they may.

3. The selfless partner will expect their mate to have some flaws, but will help the partner work on these in an accepting way. Becoming selfless involves the acknowledgment that no partner will be "perfect," and it's really okay to bond with someone who has a lot of great qualities, but not necessarily *every* ideal quality.

4. They will retain their own individuality in a relationship, and not put their partner in a superior role. This represents a basic level of self-respect, as they won't allow themselves to be pushed around. The selfless partner strives to be an equal and realizes that their partner is not the total answer to life's problems.

5. Finally, and most important, they accept the fact that *many* relationship conflicts don't have a right or wrong answer. Relationships are complex, and most of the time hover somewhere in the gray zone. There isn't one set of rules that must be followed, and the attempt to find an absolute solution to all of life's obstacles is an unproductive and selfish endeavor! The selfless partner will sometimes "agree to disagree" with their mate, and then work to reach a reasonable compromise that can at least partially satisfy both people. Isn't this the reward and challenge of a relationship—to create your own unique bond and wing it as you go?

The lesson to be learned from this reality is that your partner will never do everything exactly the way you like it. They may not handle your kids the way you want, they may show affection in a way entirely different from you, and they may hold on to some beliefs about the world that you think are just plain screwy. But please don't try to make them change their core essence. Sometimes they're going to do things the way that they like, and you're going to do things the way that you like. If you butt heads and have to come up with a compromise, at least you're talking to each other and creating some relationship energy. After all, life wouldn't be too much fun if your partner didn't drive you crazy once in a while.

CHAPTER 10

Serious Relationship Problems Require Therapy

I UNDERSTAND THAT THIS MESSAGE IS SOMETHING THAT you don't want to hear, but it's definitely a subject that needs to be addressed.

We live in an age of instant gratification, where our needs are usually met immediately. We want something, we get it. As a result, it's only natural to assume that our love relationships should work in the same way. If we have a serious relationship problem, we fix it easily and efficiently.

However, the tenth **Relationship Reality** is this:

> *Serious relationship problems require therapy.
> There's no substitute for a process that helps you
> understand the root of your relationship conflicts.
> Relationships aren't simple, and there are no simple answers*

Serious relationship problems absolutely require therapy. You're making a huge mistake if you believe that significant problems will disappear without hard work and introspection—by both you and your partner. Sure, you may be able to sweep these issues under the rug for a time, but they'll continue to build up until you trip over them again. Chronic anger, resentment, and disrespect will be almost guaranteed to ruin your relationships. I've heard numerous couples naively tell me, "We'll work it out on our own," and then they split up shortly thereafter.

Is It Serious?

First, let's define a crucial relationship concern. I'm not talking about an argument over who's going to cook dinner tonight. Common sense dictates that serious problems will involve issues such as infidelity, sexual problems, abuse (either emotional or physical), dishonesty, apathy/loss of interest in a partner, breakdowns in communication, or major disagreements about children or finances. There aren't any easy answers to these dilemmas—you and your partner are shortchanging each other if you think otherwise.

So what should you do if, for instance, your marriage is crumbling? Or if you've engaged in a string of unfulfilling relationships that don't last? What if you're simply saddened by the direction your life has taken? I strongly believe that the *best* way you can effect lasting change is to engage in a process called *therapy*.

What Therapy Is . . . and What It Isn't

Does the word *therapy* scare you off? Most people tell me that if they go into therapy, it must mean that they've given up and have completely lost control of their lives. This is an unfortunate perception, because therapy is a process that will lead to *understanding*. I can think of no downside to comprehending *why* you're doing the things you're doing and feeling the things you're feeling in a relationship. In fact, the upside is tremendous—you get a chance to make long-term changes that are sustained over time, even if you ultimately end up with a different partner.

It's notable that most of us only have a vague idea of what transpires in a psychiatrist's office, and what we do know comes courtesy of Hollywood. These movies or TV shows usually involve big stars portraying psychiatrists (or other types of therapists) and handling the juiciest of problems, from multiple personality disorders to attempted suicides. Then there's the haunting image of the mental hospital in *One Flew Over the Cuckoo's Nest.* . . . Of course, it wouldn't be nearly as entertaining to show a doctor sitting across from a patient in a nondescript office, simply discussing why the person's life seems empty and meaningless or how they're struggling with a difficult relationship issue. But that's what therapy is—it's work; and it's not glamorous, easy, or quick.

So before we move on to Part II (which is devoted to the issues we'd discuss if you were actually sitting in my office) and start our own brand of relationship therapy, I feel the need to discuss some of the other approaches you may have tried to solve your relationship conflicts. Some of these techniques might have worked for you to an extent, and some probably didn't help at all. My feeling is that *none* of the following methods will, in and of themselves, lead to a fundamental and sustained change in your relationship—especially if it's on the verge of collapsing.

1. "Pop Psychology" Is Usually Not Therapy

Although there are some brilliant and thought-provoking pop psychology books on the market, for the most part, most of them fall short of helping you actually change your life. They may provide some very nice tips on dating, the differences between men and women, communication, or how to find that "right" partner, but ultimately, none of them offer real solutions for you if you're in serious relationship trouble. In the final analysis, their solutions are usually short-lived, because they don't address *why* you're doing certain things based on your individual life experiences.

It's analogous to making that New Year's resolution (again!) to work out and lose weight. You maintain an emotional high for two weeks of health-club visits . . . and then you don't go back to the club again for the rest of the year. Then next year, you're right back in the same situation because you never took the time to figure out *why* you're overweight in the first place, or why you simply don't enjoy working out consistently. Appeals to your emotions can only carry you so far, because emotional "cheerleading" ("I'm really gonna do it this time!") can't possibly overcome thought processes that have been wired into your brain for years.

2. "Advice" Isn't Therapy

The other day, I was watching a daytime talk show, and it challenged viewers to "follow your heart" and "capture your internal power." We were being told that we would need to take control of our anger issues and channel this negative energy into assertive action. This advice, of course, sounded great, and on the surface certainly has tremendous potential, but it's not relationship therapy. Why? Because no techniques were offered to help the viewer understand *where* this anger originated from or what caused it in the first place. According to my principles of relationship therapy that will be described later, a true change can only take place after the old behavior or emotion is understood in a systematic way. Anything short of this will probably only lead to partial or temporary change. Moreover, a catchy phrase such as "Capture your internal power!" is too vague for me, and certainly too hard to define.

Similarly, advice from family and friends isn't therapy either. Over the years, many clients have come in to my office and related that they finally got to the point that they "needed" to see me. When I asked them why it took so long, most of them gave me a variation on the same theme, which was: "I thought I could get some advice from my friends and that would help."

Now I'm sure that you also have many well-intentioned friends and relatives who are eager to put in their two cents regarding your life. Mom and Dad, brothers and sisters, best friends, or even casual acquaintances will, if given half a chance, offer up opinions and advice. The nice thing about these discussions is that they involve people who are usually caring, supportive, and concerned about what happens to you. But generally, their feedback isn't objective, which often leads to solutions based on minimizing pain and making everyone happy, while keeping you from facing the tough decisions that may lead to even greater happiness in the long run. Their emotions about your partner or relationship may also enter the equation—then you end up making a decision based on what *they want* rather than what *you need* to do.

3. A Sense of Morality Isn't True Relationship Therapy

This is a complicated and usually divisive issue, because a lot of people live their lives according to what they *should* do in their love relationships, instead of what *needs* to be done. There's no doubt that this approach has been pushed into our national consciousness in the past few years due to one person: radio personality Dr. Laura Schlessinger.

There's no disputing the fact that she's done a great job of marketing herself as an expert on personal relationships and questions of morality. She's capitalized on the tried-and-true media secret that *controversy and radical ideas = publicity = ratings = a better chance that she'll stay on the air.* You may have listened to Dr. Laura or read her books and maybe you even agree with some of her advice. After all, who can disagree with themes of "family values," "doing the right thing," and proper parenting?

What's really unfortunate, though, is that many listeners come to believe that Dr. Laura is engaging in therapy, when in fact, most of her answers are rooted in moralistic religious beliefs and/or political views. Even the title of "doctor" can be misleading, as you would naturally expect her to be a psychologist or psychiatrist, but she's not. Then again, her life itself is a mass of contradictions that she rationalizes in a "do as I say and not as I've done" mentality. Furthermore, it's painfully evident to me that she has had little formal training in psychology or psychiatry. During my training to become a doctor, I learned that effective communication between therapist and client is rooted in an empathic approach toward the person asking for help.

A good therapist won't berate or belittle their client in an attempt to effect change. Respect is one of the most basic expectations that a client should have in terms of their relationship with their therapist. Whether you like Dr. Laura or not, one thing can't be overlooked: Her hardcore approach may provide voyeuristic entertainment to the audience as she hammers on a caller, but it will only be marginally helpful to someone with a real relationship crisis. Managing a relationship is simply too complex to be reduced to her technique, which implies, "I'm right and know what's good for you." The next time that you see or hear her in the media, ask yourself the questions: "Who made her an expert?" and "Why does she need to set up an unequal power dynamic with callers in which she's the all-knowing parental figure and they're the child who needs to be educated?"

The answer to the first question is: *She* did. The answer to the second question is: Because on some level, this probably feels comfortable to her.

Of course, this commentary is just my opinion about what doesn't work for people struggling with a difficult relationship question. I don't think that what Dr. Laura is doing on the radio is particularly helpful, but she would probably disagree with my approach, too. But that's okay with me. We both do a live call-in radio show dealing with relationship and family issues. But that's where the similarities end, both in content and delivery.

Finally, I do need to say at this point that morality is of course absolutely essential as a foundation for benevolent and generous actions by an individual, as well as a society. Without a sense of morality, there is lawlessness, unconscionable behavior, and disregard for other human beings. Even though most of us know these things, some of us break our own moral codes and ruin our lives. We do this because negative beliefs and life experiences can sometimes overpower morality. As a general code for living, however, morality can't help you understand why you're doing certain things in your relationships, and thus may be only minimally helpful in promoting real change.

A Summary of the Relationship Realities

So we've made it to the end of Part I! I urge you to give considerable thought to these concepts, even if you disagree on some of the specifics. I believe that there are certain things in life and relationships that just *are*, no matter how hard you try to rationalize it the other way. While the rest of the book will be devoted entirely to helping you understand the reasons for your relationship choices and behaviors, it may be useful to list these realities again:

1. You are the creator of your relationship. It's a valuable possession that you own.

2. There is no set of relationship rules that you must follow. The work to understand your relationship is what's really important.

3. You must stop living in a fantasy world, just hoping that things will somehow change for the better in your relationships. Change will only occur if you *do something*. Take action and set your limits.

4. What you allow to happen in your relationship is what you're going to get. Defining what you need and claiming your power is a critical step in maximizing your happiness.

5. If you need to work really hard early in the relationship, then there may be big problems down the road. Get off the relationship roller coaster.

6. If you need something, the only way to get it will be to tell your partner. No one can read your mind.

7. The right timing is a crucial factor in determining whether a particular relationship will progress. Just because *you're* ready doesn't mean that a potential partner will move at the same speed.

8. A relationship with a shaky foundation will probably not get better with the addition of children.

9. You can't always get what you want in any relationship. Great relationships happen as a result of both partners developing selfless attitudes.

10. Serious relationship problems require therapy. There's no substitute for a process that helps you understand the root of your relationship conflicts. Relationships aren't simple, and there are no simple answers.

With that, let's move on to Part II, so you can develop a new way of thinking about your partner and yourself. This will revolutionize the way that you approach your love relationships! If you learn what's driving these negative patterns, you'll be well on your way to creating *a relationship that could last a lifetime*. Join me in my office, so to speak, as we do some important relationship therapy together.

Part II

Relationship Therapy

CHAPTER 11

Relationship Therapy That Will Work for You

YOU CAN CHANGE THE DYNAMICS OF YOUR RELATIONSHIP—
it's not too late.

There's no reason why your love relationship can't be all that you've ever dreamed of. Imagine that you and your partner are so connected that you never again have to worry about the relationship falling apart, so it becomes synonymous with happiness. . . .

But is it really possible? Can *any* two people create and maintain a great relationship? You may not think so, because in your search for love, you've only met with failure and disappointment. In fact, if you're like a lot of my friends and patients, you may have given up completely. You may have come to expect that *any* love relationship you have will end up being quite painful—nothing will ever change and you'll never get what you really need. It would be really sad for you to go through life with this attitude, because things don't have to be this way.

So, you've reached a fork in the road. You can continue to head down the path you're on, which promises to be easy because your inertia is already pushing you in this direction. You won't have to make any changes whatsoever. The problem, though, is that the old way will be tantamount to a lifetime filled with frustrating relationships and bad choices. But, hey, it will be easy, so many of you will just keep floating down this path . . . complaining all the way.

But there's another route you can take. However, a journey down this avenue promises to be much harder and perhaps slower going. Yet when you've reached the end, the rewards could be tremendous. It's just that the process to get there will require much more effort on your part. This path will also challenge you to uncover the *real* issues in your relationship—some of which, I'm sure, you'd rather not even think about.

What will your decision be? Take a few moments to think about this, because you may not make a more important choice in your life. Will it be more of the same or a change for the better? Will you take the easy way out, or will you make the commitment to do some hard work?

If you've chosen the first way—the easier route—then you might as well put down this book and stop reading right now. You're on the path of least resistance, and you have no desire to find out what really makes you tick.

But if, in fact, you've chosen the second path—the longer and harder route—you've just entered my office and are willing to engage in the process of *relationship therapy*. You're going to learn to *understand* your relationships and partners in an entirely different way. You'll be giving yourself a chance to change what you've been doing for many years. *You're going to see what it really takes to make a love relationship work for you.*

In upcoming chapters, we'll look at crucial relationship concepts such as power, betrayal, honesty, trust, anger, love, communication, and unselfishness. Your experiences in life and love can only improve. And your eyes will be opened to a happy relationship—one you thought could only exist in your dreams.

What Is Relationship Therapy?

If *relationship therapy* is the best choice for allowing you to achieve fulfillment and peace in your life, then exactly what is this process? Are you destined to spend numerous hours on a psychiatrist's couch trying to figure out where you went wrong in a broken relationship?

The answer to this question is "not necessarily"— although if the pain or unhappiness is too severe, you may require actual sessions with a trained therapist. Hopefully, by looking at your relationship in a different way (as outlined in the rest of this book), you'll be able to acquire the skills you need to become your *own* relationship therapist.

By this I mean that you'll have the ability to *self-correct.* You'll learn how to eliminate old behaviors that cause things to fall apart! This is one of the greatest gifts that you can give yourself. Wouldn't it be nice to say, "I'm trying to defeat myself again, but now I can change this course *by myself*"? You may never again feel the need to say, "I can't believe I did that!"

The best part is that you will have done it yourself. After all, even if you go into real talk therapy, the goal should always be to eventually become your own master at being happy. If a licensed therapist ever tells you otherwise—that relationship therapy should be a process with no end in sight or that it will take a lifetime to figure out your problems—then that person either wants a lifelong customer or is simply misguided in their approach. My definition of *relationship therapy* doesn't mean "for the rest of your life."

Therefore, the underlying theme that permeates this principle (and which will be utilized from here on out) is:

> *Relationship therapy is the process of learning crucial relationship concepts and then understanding the unconscious reasons why we follow certain negative patterns in life and in our love relationships. After we've come to this realization, we can then develop new and productive coping skills.*

As you can see from this definition, I believe that a lot of what we do on a day-to-day basis is *unconscious* and *automatic*—stemming from reasons that we usually don't understand. If we're lucky and have had enough positive life experiences throughout our childhood and subsequent adult relationships, then these automatic ways of coping may serve us well. Our marriage succeeds, we choose compatible and stable life partners, we have an inherent sense of worth and stability, people like us, and we move forward and grow.

If, however, the past was filled with disappointment, unrealized potential, or examples of unsatisfying relationships, then we'll most likely continue to live out this cycle of defeating actions. Even if we intellectually realize that this pattern is harmful, we'll continue to do what we know! So *any* therapy—whether it's done with an actual therapist or by reading a book—must have the goal of *understanding* at its roots. We can then change these automatic negative behaviors into newly formed positive actions that will enhance our relationships.

I've seen many patients over the years enter therapy and say, "Just fix me!" I have to remind them that this isn't a "fixing" process—because that would, by necessity, make me impose my own beliefs on them and not allow real growth to occur. Their life choices and patterns have to be based upon something, and this something must be put into context and understood for them to have a chance at better relationships. *There's simply no shortcut.* Understanding who you are is a struggle, but it's a battle worth fighting. Doing anything less than this is a disservice to you and those around you.

You may have had a decent upbringing, with parents who did their very best for you; perhaps there were no major traumas or losses, or any one particular moment that defined the rest of your life. Maybe you can't see an obvious reason why you haven't found happiness in your relationships, but somehow it's not happening as you envisioned. You can't seem to locate the answers that will bring everything together.

Don't give up, or become angry that you're not getting what you deserve. Understanding is a journey, and if you're curious enough about where it could lead, then you can move ahead.

The Core Principles of Relationship Therapy

First, there are certain basic concepts about managing a relationship that you must understand. You've probably never taken a course that has forced you to look at these issues, so think of the rest of this book as that course, one that will give you a "relationship education."

Let's take a look at the following four relationship principles:

Core Principle #1—Your Past Sets the Stage for Every Single Thing That Happens in Your Life

Like it or not, you can't escape your past. Recently, I saw a movie in which one of the recurring messages was: *You may be through with the past, but the past may not be through with you.* This is prophetic, and very true. Your memories and experiences matter, and they set the stage for *everything* you do in life. The partners you pick, the relationships you create, the jobs you choose—it's all based on past experiences. If you don't believe me, then evaluate some of your friends who have ended up in unhappy relationships. I'll bet you can see that they never understood their pasts, and they're repeating old patterns over and over—which brings us to the next point.

Core Principle #2—If You Don't Understand Your Past, You're Destined to Repeat Previous Failures

I should say that you're *doomed* to repeat old mistakes, because you'll continue to pick the same types of partners, make the same poor job decisions, and end up in the same unfulfilling situations in your life. The pattern is set in place, leading you to spiral downward in a vicious circle of destructive decisions, unless you follow the next principle.

Core Principle #3—You Must Begin to Process an "Objective Analysis" of Your Life

You don't need to relive every experience or memory in detail, but you must start to look objectively at previous relationships in your life, including the ones you've had with your parents, siblings, family members, friends, *and* people you've dated. This includes an analysis of the positive *and* negative points of these experiences. (I'll help you do this in a later chapter.) This means that you need to make the commitment to look inside yourself—most people are quite frightened to do so. Sometimes patients will walk into my office on day one and say that they can't handle the process of talking about their life because it's too painful. So, they avoid the tough conversations with themselves and their partners.

I tell them that my hope is that by looking within, they'll enrich themselves and become more free. A key to good mental health is looking *inward* for the answers, rather than depending on others to provide direction, for what happens if they don't have the right answers and you decide to follow their advice? One of the primary concepts people with successful relationships know is: *In order to understand another person, you first have to take a good look inside yourself.* These individuals are aware that in order to do so, they have to follow their hearts—but it's also necessary to use their brains and logistical skills in addition to their emotions.

Core Principle #4—Your Relationship Therapy Begins with Your Asking "Why?"

How do you go about looking within? First, you must be curious about your and your partner's motivations in the relationship. A real therapist asks "Why?": *Why are you doing that? Why are you embarking on this path? Why are you feeling this?*

Likewise, your challenge as your own therapist will be to also ask those (and other) questions of yourself, and frequently. *Why did I feel like that? Why did I get angry with my spouse? Why didn't I do the household chores when I said I would? Why did I choose an incompatible partner again? Why am I attracted to a certain type of person? Why am I never happy? Why do I feel as if I never get what I want out of a relationship?* The list of questions could go on and on, but approaching your relationship in this way can lead to some wonderful and productive discussions between you and your partner.

Now you're probably asking, "So how am I going to start doing this? I don't think that way!" I'll counter with my belief that you *can* think in this way if you put your mind to it, because the alternative is to be ignorant about what's driving your relationships. A practice of questioning will lead to a true understanding of your current relationship and previous experiences in life. Understanding leads to control about relationship choices, which leads to true freedom to make rational and positive decisions. All of this flows from the habit of using the word *why* in your daily relationship interactions.

I want you to keep this paradigm in mind throughout the rest of the book, because it's a part of every topic we're going to cover from here on out:

> *Asking why* ⟶ *leads to an understanding of previous life experiences and current relationship issues* ⟶ *leads to true control* ⟶ *allows freedom to create a positive relationship.*

The most important *why* questions that I want you to keep in mind throughout every day of your relationship are these:

- Why am I with this particular partner, and why am I in this particular love relationship?

- Why do I allow my partner to do certain things that upset me or make our relationship difficult?

- Why don't I get what I need out of our interactions?

- Why do I exhibit behaviors and emotions that could potentially end the relationship?

I know that at this point you may not have the answers to these questions, but the next thought that ought to follow any *why* question should be an answer that begins with "Because I . . ." This process forces you to think about your motives and behavior in the relationship, and from this will come an understanding of your choices.

What Happens to People Who Resist Relationship Therapy

Let's look at a couple of examples of people who didn't comprehend what it takes to have a good connection, and who didn't understand why they'd been following certain repetitive patterns in their relationships.

Tammy

Tammy had been married for about three years and was the mother of two young children. She called my radio show because her husband had left her suddenly. Tammy later found out that he'd been cheating on her. However, she wasn't calling the show to cope with this loss.

This is what she inquired: "How can I get him back? If I can somehow bring him back to me, my life would be wonderful again."

I replied, "What do you mean, 'get him back'? Why do you want this guy?"

Tammy answered, "Because I love him!"

I said, "I don't think what you're feeling is love. What you're experiencing is some kind of past baggage that you've brought into this current relationship, because obviously, this isn't a man who's capable of making you happy. You're becoming a victim."

As I let her talk, I found out that, in fact, Tammy *was* a victim and this was a long-standing personality trait for her. She'd always chosen men who victimized and left her, but she didn't see it that way. The only thing in her mind was getting the abuser back because she'd been taught that any relationship was better than none at all. Tammy had also seen important people in her life mistreat each other as she grew up. But until we spoke, she'd never taken the time to understand what had happened in her life that caused her to interact in this way. Yet, despite learning this about her own psychology, she didn't seem particularly interested in learning more about herself. Consequently, I'm sure that Tammy continues to have terrible relationships.

Steve

Steve was a man I consulted with years ago. He dated regularly, always juggling several women at once. He was very popular and could be counted on to be present at the biggest social events in town, yet he complained to me that he never quite felt fulfilled.

He constantly complained about the women he was seeing: "She's not quite right," "She doesn't dress well," "She's not funny (or intelligent or pretty) enough."

Finally, I asked, "Don't you think *you* have anything to do with this? You're the one who keeps choosing these women. You're the one making the decision to go out with them, and you keep going out with the same type of woman over and over. Essentially, you're dating clones. Why do you keep doing this?"

Steve's answer was, "I don't know why I'm doing it."

I said, "Well, why don't you find out? Let's try to get to the root of *why* you keep choosing these women who are unavailable and distant, and with whom you have little chance of a real connection."

Steve had never thought of himself in this way before, but it was the key to unlocking the door to why he had repeatedly made the same relationship mistakes. With time, and a lot of hard work, he was able to break his cycle of unsatisfying relationships.

For every Tammy or Steve, there are countless others who have never taken the time to understand why they're following maladaptive patterns and haven't ever really been happy. People like that will continue to struggle through unpleasant relationships without ever managing to pinpoint why it always goes wrong. *They've never taken the time to work through these difficult situations in relationship therapy.*

The topics described in this book could immensely help *both* Tammy and Steve—two people who exhibit seemingly unrelated problems—because *the principles of my relationship therapy are universal.* These aren't concepts that apply specifically to one situation or person—they apply to anyone. I say this with confidence because every single one of us has a past—experiences that, unless critically analyzed, will catch up to us. This is where our "emotional baggage" comes from.

Why Do I Need a New Relationship Approach?

Since I've just dared you to ask yourself "why" several times each day, it's only fair that you challenge me on the concept of relationship therapy: Is it really needed? Why can't most of us just wing it and hope that everything turns out okay? After all, many people find that perfect partner and enjoy a satisfying, healthy relationship— but most of these people aren't reading this book, and *you are.* I have to make the assumption that you're not doing so well.

Incredibly, a lot of marriages are doomed to split up—in the United States today, approximately half of all marriages end in divorce. That's an amazing statistic. Sadly enough, this shows that people can't hold relationships together—even if they do, there's more trouble on the horizon. Several studies indicate that a large percentage of men will cheat on their partner at some point.

Women reading this book are probably thinking, *Oh, those men! What jerks! I can't believe that they cheat on their wives.* But hold on a minute—the same studies indicate that at least 20 to 30 percent of all women in committed relationships will cheat on their husbands. The same research has also cited a huge percentage of people in the U.S. who have said that they're not happy in their current relationship, and given the opportunity, probably wouldn't marry the same person again.

Changing the Old Ways

So what has happened in our society? You probably heard your parents say, "Back in the good ol' days, no one ever got divorced." Mom and Dad may have been married for 50 years, and Grandma and Grandpa for 60. It appeared as if they had very happy relationships—did they know some secret that we don't know now? Did they just stay together even if they hated each other? Or were divorce attorneys simply not as available as they are today?

There could be a lot of different explanations, but I believe the one that makes the most sense is that we move more quickly now. Sometimes both partners have to work many hours a day, almost every day of the week. We've moved away from our roots and our families, and while this leads to more opportunities to meet greater numbers of people, it also leads to more temptations to stray. It's easy to avoid communicating with someone you love, easy to drift apart, and just as easy to leave or get a quick divorce. We now think, *If this doesn't work or it's too much work, I can end it quickly.*

I sincerely hope this isn't the case. I can't fathom that everyone who starts a relationship has a fantasy that they'll probably get divorced and move on to someone else, but regardless of what people think on the way *in* to a relationship, it's doubtful that they realize that they're already starting out at a disadvantage. They've probably never truly analyzed the strengths, weaknesses, and patterns that they exhibit in intimate relationships.

Did you actually take a relationship course before you started dating or got married? *Did you and your partner talk with someone about how you would make your relationship work, even in the difficult times?* I highly doubt that you did. If you were lucky, you went to your local church and spoke to a counselor—maybe you even took a personality test. Before we got married, my wife and I went to our church and took one. We answered all of the questions, and two weeks later, we were told that we were compatible and that we could get married.

We were fortunate—at least we got to analyze some test results. But most people never even go this far. They don't really scrutinize themselves and their partner before they commit to a long-term relationship. It's not because they're lazy. Most people simply don't think of doing these things before committing. It's not romantic to talk about potential problems with your mate, for it shatters the illusion that "love will find a way."

So couples muddle along, hoping that things will somehow turn out all right, living through all of the fights and arguments, waiting forever for their day in the sun—which never comes. Maybe they end up sleeping in the same bed night after night, never touching each other. Or perhaps they put all of their energy into the children. Or maybe they just give up and never find true relationship happiness.

I hope this hasn't happened to you. But if you're unhappy with the way things are right now, then have the courage to find a real sense of peace and freedom. Move ahead with the first thing you'll need to accomplish in relationship therapy: It's time to develop the habit of *looking inside* yourself for some definitive answers.

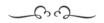

CHAPTER 12

Take a Good Look Inside

SOMETIMES THERE SEEMS TO BE NO MEANING TO THE world. Bad things happen to good people; good things happen to bad people. Consequently, our path becomes clouded, and we don't know which way to turn.

We think that "finding the answers in life" will guarantee success. Politicians understand that we are always questing for answers, so they claim to know the very thing that will improve the quality of our lives—then they promise to deliver it. The mass media reports the opinions of "experts" who glibly offer up suggestions on how to live, what to buy, who to believe, and how to behave. Even product advertisements subliminally give the impression that *"our* way of thinking is better for you than *their* way."

On a smaller scale, each day thousands of people plead dejectedly with their partners, "Just tell me what to do!" *In essence, we give our power away.* Maybe we *want* to give it away—sometimes it's easier to be told what to do, just like when we were children. A successful relationship, however, isn't founded on what someone else has to say. Unsuccessful people never understand this concept, so they go through life depending on others to supply the answers and enhance their lives. They don't comprehend that *the first step to better relationships is taking a look inside for their own answers.* Confronting your own weaknesses can only make you stronger. This is also the first major step in our relationship therapy.

Move Forward, or Stay Put?

I'd like to share a couple of stories with you on the topic of looking inside.

Anita

Anita was very unhappy when she came in to my office. She'd suffered a very traumatic childhood, as her mother had abandoned the family when the children were very young—so Anita was left to raise her younger brothers and sisters. Anita eventually left home and entered into a relationship that turned out to be extremely abusive—it ended, but she then went through a string of similar relationships with controlling, mean-spirited men. In her early 30s, she came to me and said, "You've got to help me. I don't know what to do. I'm having bad luck with relationships, and I really want to make a difference in my life."

So I began to see Anita in therapy. I discovered very early on that she was quite scared about looking into herself and her past. Sometimes she would clam up completely and not speak about anything of substance that had occurred in her life. But even though it was difficult and provoked some intense anxiety in her, she kept trying to understand her life. I prompted her with my belief that understanding wouldn't lead to more pain, but keeping her misery inside would eventually erode her soul. I didn't tell her what to do—in fact, I usually didn't even give advice. I'd simply rephrase her statements and say, "The reason you've made certain decisions is always about understanding."

Anita invested the time and energy to look inside, which took a lot of courage, especially when it seemed as if there would be no end to her pain. Little by little, Anita began to develop the ability to become her own relationship expert.

The outcome was a happy ending, as Anita's relationships have vastly improved, and she doesn't spend her days despondent and depressed. It was a frightening and time-consuming process for her to ask, *"Who am I, and why am I feeling this way?"* It certainly wasn't easy for her to revisit the unhappy experiences from her past, but, in making sense of these issues, Anita was able to find some peace.

🦆 🦆 🦆

Not all relationship therapy is so successful, as this next patient will illustrate. (I generally see equal amounts of men and women in my practice, but this case involves another woman.)

Brenda

Brenda would come in weekly to talk about her problems, and at the end of the sessions, she'd usually say something to the effect of: "Okay, I've told you everything. What do you think I should do? Tell me what to do."

I resisted giving her advice. Instead, I would reply, "Let's talk about why you feel the need for me to give you all the answers."

This didn't feel comfortable to her because she'd always been told what to do as a child. Brenda's parents had told her exactly how to behave and feel, and what was right and wrong. Therefore, it was natural that she would expect me to give her direction, which she would then obediently follow—since that was the way it was between her and everyone else in her life. Brenda was a great follower, but she became paralyzed when challenged to think on her own. In fact, the reason she entered therapy in the first place was because she had a husband who set all the rules in the relationship and told her exactly what to do.

On the one hand, that felt pretty good to Brenda. She was uncomfortable making decisions, so she naturally gravitated toward people who would do that for her. In this way, she could avoid looking inside. But the other side of this coin was that she got stuck with controlling partners—she'd traded power for ease. Because I wouldn't assume the dominant role that she'd forced others into, she'd become quite frustrated with me—she'd miss sessions and relate to me in an angry manner. I was undeterred, and kept talking with her about the dynamic she naturally established with others, which allowed them to guide her on any life decision she might make.

We seemed to be making some progress on this concept, but then an interesting thing happened. After each session, Brenda would return home and tell her husband about it. He would then discourage further therapy, telling her that I didn't know what I was talking about. What he was really communicating was his absolute terror of her gaining more power and self-esteem, because that would upset their established balance of power. He didn't want her to change, as this would lessen his authority.

Can you guess the outcome? Unfortunately for Brenda, she eventually dropped out of therapy. I couldn't help her because she regressed back into the pattern of allowing someone else to make life decisions for her. She'd given all the power to her husband—and he readily seized it. Unlike Anita (from the previous story), Brenda was unable to find the courage and strength to look within for answers. She could never confront her weaknesses.

I don't know what became of her, but I'm sure she's still unhappy, still subject to the whims of others.

Giving Away Your Relationship Power
(Without Even Knowing It)

Do other people have the right to impose their own will and beliefs on you? Unless you're incarcerated, I know of no law that gives others the absolute authority to do so. The only way they can claim this power is if *you give it to them!* Why would this happen? Do you think that others have read a rule book that you didn't even know existed? Do you feel that they must certainly have all the answers, since they act so confidently and you're so full of doubt and insecurity?

If your husband says, "Here's what we're going to do," or if your wife says, "Honey, here's what you have to do," should you reactively fall in line? Do you simply choose to avoid potential arguments and conflicts at any cost? The bottom line is that *this way of living leads to a passive, dependent stance and a victim mentality.* True freedom is sacrificed, as you become a pawn in someone else's way of thinking.

You may internally deny that you've ever given your power away. You could be saying to yourself, "Wait a minute—I don't let other people make decisions about my life. I don't fit into this category."

Let's use a very common situation to see if you do indeed give your power away. For example, have you ever been with someone and the two of you can't even decide where to go for dinner?

You ask your partner, "Where do you want to go?"

He or she replies, "I don't know. Where do *you* want to go?"

You respond, " I don't know either."

After going back and forth in this manner several times, you both look at each other with exasperation, realizing that you've just totally wasted your time and energy. You didn't accomplish a thing—on an issue as simple as selecting a restaurant.

That's just a small example of how we sometimes unwittingly give away our power. The next time your partner asks, "Where do you want to go for dinner?" take the lead, say what kind of food you want, and then make a decision.

You may be assuming the passive stance reflexively—after all, it's easier to have a decision come from an external source than an internal one. If you take a stand and behave according to what you think is reasonable, it's always possible that the other person may take exception to your position. We all inherently strive to be liked and admired because it feels good. It's also difficult to face the consequences of being disliked or rejected, so you back off from your position or cave in to the other person. Consequently, *if you walk through life afraid of asserting your own power and making tough decisions, I can almost guarantee that you're afraid that people will be angry with you.* You may also fear that others will think that you're foolish or stupid—if this is the case, it's imperative that you begin to understand the origins of this tendency.

Stop Going Around in Circles!

How many times has the following happened to you?

You're upset about something in your relationship. Your partner, who isn't completely insensitive to your moods, asks, "What's wrong?"

You meekly say, "Oh, nothing. It's no big deal."

"Tell me," they encourage.

You answer, "No. It's stupid. Just forget it."

The conversation goes nowhere, so the feeling gets buried back into your subconscious and you walk away unsatisfied. Yet you *had* the opening—your partner encouraged free expression, but you just couldn't say how you really felt. You were afraid of sounding like a complainer, or worried that only negativity would arise out of the interaction. Maybe you felt that they wouldn't respect your feelings or that nothing would change anyway, so you backed down.

Think about the loss that occurs when you engage in this type of interaction. You're not free—you're trapped, unable to fully express yourself. *You're most likely replaying an old pattern from the past in which your thoughts were never legitimized by your parents, or perhaps you saw them behaving in this way toward each other.*

Consequently, free expression is squashed. You learn to ignore your true feelings, and they get bottled up inside. The problem, though, is that these feelings and impulses will find their way out in other ways.

The Circular Paradigm Becomes:

Looking for
answers externally

leads to a
passive,
dependent
stance

now you're
alone again

leads to loss
of power

which leads to
the destruction of
the relationship

so you try to regain
control through
self-defeating
measures

leading you to
feel apathy or
anger/resentment

Unfortunately for a lot of people, this circle will repeat itself over and over, precipitating a series of unfulfilling relationships. The critical point in the cycle is this: *You must start to develop the ability to tell others what you're feeling or what you want.* It's truly okay to do this. However, verbalizing your internal desires doesn't mean that others will respect you, nor does it mean that they will necessarily agree with you. For instance, you may completely disagree with what I've written thus far, but I'm still going to say what I want to say because I believe in my approach to therapy and feel confident enough to know that I have something helpful to offer. By the same token, I hope that you'll generate the internal strength to make positive changes.

In the classic movie *The Wizard of Oz*, Dorothy had to discover that finding someone who she thought had all of the answers (the wizard) was ultimately not all that helpful. She came to the realization that the *process* of life and her own ability to handle obstacles was what counted. Dorothy's struggle to find her own power was what made her life worthwhile—not some search for an unattainable pot of gold over the rainbow. *The process of living, the daily struggles, the obstacles to success, and the search to look within for understanding are the things that give meaning to life.* If you embrace this process of finding your own answers, you have a chance to succeed—to become your *own* wizard. If you resist taking control of your own life, you're only going to find unrealized dreams, anxiety, disappointment, and poor guidance.

The Wizard of Oz contains another extremely important message: *The power is within.* Repeat this to yourself right now.

Then tell yourself, *"I'll stop letting others tell me what I should be doing or how I should live. I will make my own life. I am my own guide. I am the only one who can make it happen. The real answers are within me."*

Empathically Confront Your Weaknesses

Only in the context of *empathic confrontation* will you be able to develop the ability to look within for answers. This is the exact approach that I would use if you were sitting in my office struggling with a serious relationship issue. But what does this mean?

Empathy means that I strive to understand how difficult it is for you to look at your situation and feelings. Likewise, you must *tolerate* your own shortcomings—this is an absolutely critical step before you can go on to analyze your issues without being ashamed or embarrassed.

Remember Stuart Smalley, the character developed by Al Franken on *Saturday Night Live* several years ago? Stuart spent most of his time trying to overcome his numerous life problems, and he would proclaim, "I'm good enough, I'm smart enough, and doggone it, people like me!" Of course he was a parody, an exaggerated response to the entire self-help movement. But his little mantra—even though it's hilarious—also contained a message that we could all stand to hear. Sometimes saying Stuart's words silently to yourself, as silly as they may seem, can be extremely helpful. That is, you can recognize that you've suffered through some tough times and unsatisfactory relationships, but you can stop being so hard on yourself and give yourself a break.

Think about this: *You're a winner simply by making it through another day filled with challenges. You're a winner if you even try to get in touch with who you are.*

Recognizing that failure will happen is vital; how you respond to this ultimately determines your happiness. Top athletes understand this concept. Michael Jordan once did a commercial in which he recounted his dozens of failures and lost games—yet he kept going. He gave himself a break internally and didn't make himself feel like a loser. Also keep in mind that almost every artist and performer has been rejected countless times and were told they were no good, but most of them didn't pack it in—they were empathic to themselves and maintained some faith in their talent.

The clients who made the biggest gains with me all had this in common: *They stopped coming down on themselves so hard and learned that they weren't so bad after all, even after failed marriages, unsuccessful jobs, or family problems.* This freed them to objectively look at themselves, without strong emotions getting in the way.

The word *confrontation* usually scares people. I always hear a groan from an audience when I start to speak about confronting life, for the image it conjures up is always the same: Two people are yelling and screaming at each other, with no resolution to the altercation in sight. They're saying exactly what's on their minds, all right—but in a mean and vindictive way. The result is hurt feelings and egos. For most people, the fear is that confrontation means that unpleasant situations will occur between you and your partner, leading to a disabled relationship

Now, however, I want you to start thinking about confrontation and conflicts in a different light. The key is this: *When you confront yourself with the harsh reality of the decisions you've made and your subsequent actions, it doesn't necessarily mean that disagreeable things are going to happen.* If you go further and confront your partner (whether you're dating, engaged, or married) about some of the things they do that affect the relationship, does that automatically mean that everything is going to end?

My feeling is that empathic confrontation actually *improves* the relationship—it's when you *don't* tell your partner what's bothering you that the relationship suffers and ends. One given is that if you hold in your emotions, the anger will boil inside and eventually come out in some other way. For instance, little things will set you off, or you'll just withdraw into a shell. The relationship will end and you'll exclaim, "But we never fought!" The trouble is, you didn't have any *real* communication either.

Confronting Yourself

Confrontation is vital, and if done in an empathic way, it can literally save a relationship. You must use confrontation as a tool in every single interpersonal relationship in your life, especially the most important one—*the relationship with yourself.* Maybe you need to confront the fact that you sometimes don't stand up for yourself or verbalize what you want. Perhaps you should look at your tendency to search for answers outside of yourself, instead of defining your own dream. Or maybe you ought to face your partner and say, "I don't like what you're doing." This is particularly difficult, since most of us think that our partner must have a good reason for their behavior, so we back down from confrontation.

Suppose your partner is staying out too late at night, doesn't help with the household chores, or perhaps is even cheating on you. It's natural to think that there must be a good reason for their actions, so it would rock the boat to say anything negative. There have literally been hundreds of callers to my radio show over the years who play out this scenario with their partner. The conversations I have with these individuals usually go something like this:

Caller: "I found out that my husband has been cheating on me for months. He's never home, doesn't help with the children, and is really mean to me."

Me: "Have you confronted him about his behavior? Have you told him that you know?"

Caller: "No, I haven't done that yet."

Me: "Why not?"

Caller: "I don't know. Maybe it will get better if I don't say anything to upset him."

At this point, the calls always go in one of three directions: (1) The woman feels as if she is somehow to blame and therefore deserves to be hurt; (2) she believes that her husband must have a very good reason for cheating, which justifies his behavior; or (3) she thinks that if she says anything, her husband will become more upset, and *she will* have ruined the relationship.

The outcome is always the same: The wife feels trapped and helpless to change anything, and she takes on the victim role. The husband continues to cheat, the relationship eventually ends, and she comes away with the thought that she tried to be so nice and—"look what happened." Or she leaves the relationship, claiming that she had absolutely no role in its undoing, because, after all, the husband did the cheating.

What a person in this position doesn't realize is that it was *her responsibility* to confront his behavior after she found out—her failure to do so also contributed to their downfall! She'll probably go on to another relationship, where the same thing could quite possibly happen again, and her response will be the same—because she hasn't learned from her past experiences that *active communication and confrontation are crucial to the survival of a relationship*, even on matters much less important than infidelity.

Remember this important concept: *Every time you let your partner get away with something that bothers you, the relationship is one step closer to failing.* Letting small things go is one thing, but just hoping that problems will disappear is flawed thinking based on an incorrect assumption.

Renée

Another illustration of this dynamic may prove helpful. Renée, a client of mine from several years ago, complained that her husband, Alan, worked too much. He was the classic "workaholic," spending many hours of overtime at the office, which he justified for financial reasons. Alan claimed that he wanted to make their lives better . . . yet he was never home. He'd leave at 6:30 every morning and often get home after midnight. He would grunt at his wife, eat something, fall asleep, and then do the same thing all over again—seven days a week.

Initially, Renée felt pretty good about the marriage—the money was rolling in and they were considered upwardly mobile in the community. Alan also ran a big corporation, so it was a nice feeling to be married to a guy who was so industrious and respected. But after a couple of years, she started to feel neglected.

Renée asked Alan, "Is the reason you never want to be around because there's something wrong with me?"

"No. It's just the work," he assured her. "We're fine. I still love you."

Yet they only had sex every few months. He didn't help raise their children, and it got to the point that Alan and Renée rarely even spoke to each other. Not only did they not spend *any* quality time together, but she felt guilty every time she asked to see him.

Renée told me, "He's just trying to provide a good life for us."

When I then asked her if she'd ever spoken to her husband about her unhappiness in the relationship, Renée said no. I found this amazing—that even after years of marriage, she didn't feel comfortable enough to simply ask why he was working so hard. She couldn't confront him on his emotional abandonment of her and their family.

This led into a discussion of why Renée never shared her feelings with Alan. She tried to justify her passivity by making the excuse that she thought he'd "change" after he'd made enough money.

"What gives you that idea?" I challenged her. "He's been doing this for years. You really think that one day he'll just magically stop working so hard?"

She maintained that if she just hung in there long enough, it would all pay off in the end. Renée was hoping for her pot of gold over the rainbow, and was kidding herself that the relationship was fine.

Sometimes, my job is to be the voice of reason amidst the insanity, so I had to point out the harsh reality that what Renée wanted wasn't going to happen. The pattern had been allowed to go on way too long, and what we needed to discover was *how* she got into this situation in the first place.

So, I started asking her the "Why?" questions: *Why do you put your needs second? Why don't you ever challenge him? Why don't you tell him what you want in life? Why don't you share your vision of a fulfilling life with your husband?*

Renée revealed that she never really even *had* a vision. Her concept of marriage was exactly what had played out in her relationship. In her mind, married couples interacted as she and Alan had—husband gets up, goes to work, doesn't pay any attention to his wife, and everyone is unhappy. This is the dynamic she'd seen in the past—it was the way her parents had structured their marriage. Yet she held out a fading hope that Alan would change, and since she believed that women aren't supposed to question their husband's motives, she didn't intend to.

After *many* long discussions, I finally convinced her to speak up and make her feelings known. But here was the next hurdle: What if she told him how she felt and he didn't listen, or worse—didn't care? What if, despite her wishes, he ignored her and kept working just as hard?

I countered that the real gain wouldn't be an immediate change in his behavior—it would be the change in *her* behavior. No matter how Alan responded, Renée had no control over it. But she could now take the steps of starting to run her *own* life. By empathically confronting herself about why she didn't get what she needed from her husband, and why she had never asked for more, Renée was able to break her own unsatisfying circle and take her power back. Maybe using confrontation wouldn't help much in her relationship with Alan, but it could make the next one better.

Taking the Lead

It's now *your* turn to confront yourself on something I bet you do every day. You give your power away in subtle ways and depend on someone else to tell you what to do— be it telling you how to manage your life, what to do in your relationships, or how you should feel . . . it happens more often than you think.

From this moment on, *I challenge you to catch yourself every time you passively let someone make a decision for you or you actually ask someone else for advice.* This behavior isn't necessarily always negative, but it's crucial to recognize why you depend on someone else for answers.

Ask yourself, *"Why am I letting them take the lead? Am I too scared, lazy, or helpless to make my own decisions?"* You may be surprised by the answers you receive.

Every time you give away power to your partner, it establishes a pattern that makes them the boss and gives them control.

Try the following **exercise**. (You may find that carrying around a pen and a pad of paper will help with this practice.)

> Finish this sentence: *"I allowed someone else to decide . . . "*
>
> Then ask, *"Why did I allow this? I did this because . . . "*

This exercise forces you to think about the multiple ways in which you give your power away by not searching internally for what you truly desire. I think that you'll be amazed by how many times a day you unwittingly lose control of your own life. When I did this exercise myself, I was shocked by my loss of power in small, subtle ways. I found myself complaining that certain things didn't get done in my life, yet I expected others to do these things for me. From scheduling to career choices to decisions about my home, I gave the power to others and then got upset when I didn't get the desired results. I'm generally a patient person, but I became angry with others when they didn't do what I thought they should be doing. They retorted that I was essentially demanding that they read my mind! We had reached a stalemate—until I figured out that I needed to step back and ask myself *why* I expected others to take charge.

When I did so, my anxiety decreased, and I was again able to make important life decisions. (I also kept my friends in the process.) This happened because I was curious about my own behavior. Again, the cornerstone of successful therapy is a willingness to analyze your actions and ask "Why?" Everything in life makes sense. *We do nothing in life without a reason*—you may not be aware of the reason at the time, but there *is* a reason.

Sometimes external circumstances intrude into our lives without invitation. Catastrophes, deaths, losses, and just plain bad luck can occur at any time with no warning whatsoever. We're forced to react to events that seem senseless and meaningless, but fortunately, these situations are infrequent in our daily lives. *Remember, relationships are usually ruined by the little things that we* can *change.* Ignorance isn't bliss; over time, it erodes any chance for true happiness. The ignorant don't want to be enlightened—they have a blind faith that everything will somehow turn out all right.

If I were a real "wizard," my message would be that self-discovery can lead to peace. Even the attempt at understanding is a reward in and of itself.

CHAPTER 13

Defining Your
Dream Relationship

WHAT DO YOU REALLY HAVE TO GAIN IN THE ATTEMPT
to look inside for your own relationship answers?
It takes effort to start thinking about yourself and others
in an objective way, free of distortions and false hopes, so
is there genuinely a payoff in the end?

The answer is a resounding *yes,* if only for one reason:
Honest introspection is the foundation for *defining your
dream.* The vast majority of unhappy people in the world
have never accomplished this goal. They just don't know
how, or they've allowed others to define their dream for
them. Simply stated, they've sold out.

These dispirited people have never been honest with
themselves and said, "Here's the dream I've constructed,
like it or not. Whether this fits with anyone else's life plan

or not, I don't care, because this is what *I* want." If given a choice, these individuals don't lead, they follow, because it's easy and safe. If their life decisions aren't successful, they can conveniently blame someone else. Or they can stay in the same situation for years, complaining over and over— yet not taking any action whatsoever to change things.

We all know people like this. Perhaps it's the wife who stays in a loveless marriage but is well taken care of financially. Maybe it's the man who goes to the same boring and unsatisfying job for years, never taking the steps to be his own boss. It may be the individuals who publicly lie about their happiness but privately shed the tears of those who have given up on achieving a better life. These are all examples of people who pay the price for not taking an honest look at their own flaws.

Intuitively, it seems that most people would eventually recognize their failures and have nothing to lose by facing the brutal truth about themselves. In the world of recovery, this is called *hitting rock bottom*. Yet, just like the addict, there are some individuals who have lost almost everything and still can't take an honest look inside to see how they got to that point. They continue to follow the same unproductive behavior and never achieve their dreams. They honestly don't take stock of their lives because they're either scared of taking an unfamiliar path, or too embarrassed to admit that they have shortcomings.

In your own life, it's natural to want to avoid facing those characteristics that you feel will destroy you if allowed to surface. You probably think that others won't like you if you reveal your "true" self. What you don't realize, though, is that *the tendency to live in a fantasy world is the real destructive force*. Hiding behind a wall of lies consumes your ability to live up to your full potential. The dream is shattered.

So how can we keep our dreams alive? I challenge you to look at yourself and your relationships in a new way. I understand that you may not naturally know how to do so—it's easy to get confused about how to define what you truly want from a partner. It doesn't just mean that you look inside and say, "Well, I screwed that one up again!" Realize that introspection isn't a negative experience— many positive things can arise from a systematic analysis of your relationship goals.

Therefore, I'm now going to take you, step-by-step, through a series of exercises designed to help you crystallize your dreams for your love relationship. Remember that the common thread of all these exercises is an honest look inside your very self. The ultimate goal is for you to start defining what you *truly want* in a relationship! So let's get started.

Defining What Kind of Relationship You Have

There's no doubt that one of the most critical mistakes you can make in a love relationship is to not see it for what it is. I've spoken to countless people who have wasted precious time and energy on someone who has absolutely no interest in the same type of relationship. Usually, one person desires intimacy and the other just wants to be friends. One of the most dreaded things any of us can hear is that a potential love interest only desires a friendship. Yet, sometimes our response is to push even harder, believing that more effort will pay off in the end.

This approach—trying to force one type of relationship

to become another—usually leads to a lot of heartbreak. Sometimes friendships just aren't meant to evolve into romantic relationships—but it's really hard to accept this when we get emotional and our ego gets bruised.

Instead, a better (and less painful) approach would be to first understand what category the relationship falls into. *The key here is to define the relationship that you have, rather than the relationship you desperately want.*

So let's take a look at the four basic types of relationships, with the understanding that it's difficult to switch a relationship from one category to another. In fact, the attempt to force a nonromantic relationship into the romantic type will usually require a lot of effort—which may or may not be successful at the end of the day. Being honest about the people in your life—and the relationships you may or may not have with them—will bring you one step closer to finding and enjoying a relationship for a lifetime.

The following types of relationships ascend in their degree of complexity, with the final one obviously being the most complex and worthwhile.

THE FOUR BASIC TYPES OF RELATIONSHIPS

Relationship #1: Short-Term and Superficial (Not Intimate)

It's pretty obvious that this type of relationship won't develop into much. When you look back many years from now, you may not even remember it at all! But what are the features of this kind of interaction?

As the title suggests, there are some people in the world who are destined to occupy a very small part of your life, and for a very short time. I can think of some friends that I knew while growing up, as well as other people at various stages of my life, whom I called acquaintances. We moved away from each other to new places and more substantial relationships. This isn't to say that I didn't have some enjoyable times with these people—there was just no staying power. We may have had different interests and simply didn't click enough to keep the friendship going.

It's notable that none of these interactions ever really had any chance of developing into a more serious relationship, because there was no spark or hint of romance whatsoever. There was no connection made, but not a lot of effort was exerted either.

Are there any people in your life who fit into this category?

Relationship #2: Long-Term and Superficial (Not Intimate)

I can think of many people whom I've known for years who occupy a comfortable place in my life—occasionally we correspond and see each other socially. We're never going to share the most intimate details of our lives, but there's definitely a bond.

Would I make the mistake of thinking that I could possibly have a romantic relationship with these people? Probably not, because there's no depth to the feelings generated in our interactions. These relationships can certainly be rewarding, but only on a superficial level.

Just remember that many long relationships never develop into real intimacy. Although I care about my acquaintances, I don't tend to think about them on a daily basis, nor have I invested in an emotional experience with them.

Who in your life falls into this type of relationship? For instance, you may have many friends of the opposite sex whom you like to have around, but whom you would never consider in any romantic sense.

Relationship #3: Short-Term and Deep (Intimate)

I like to affectionately call this category "the road to pain." We've all fallen hard for someone, invested our emotions quickly, and then got crushed when the relationship ended just as fast. I've come to believe that when things heat up almost immediately, watch out—because the whole thing will probably fall apart even more rapidly, leaving us heartbroken and wondering why it didn't last past a few months (or weeks!).

Each of us has probably had a few shooting stars in our lives. The flame burns brightly, but then, for whatever reason, it goes out, never to be lit again. The problem is that we want that fire to keep on burning indefinitely . . . but our partner doesn't.

I can't tell you each specific reason why you've been through an intense, but short-lived, intimate relationship. Maybe the timing wasn't right, or perhaps your partner lost interest or found someone else, or it could be that they just weren't destined to be "the one."

But I do know this: I've seen many people continue to torture themselves in an attempt to keep a relationship like this going long after the handwriting was on the wall. These individuals simply can't accept the fact that *some romantic, intense relationships simply won't lead to a lifelong commitment.*

So what do you do when your dream relationship crumbles into pieces—when your partner declares, "It's over!" . . . and then finds someone else?

First, cry all you want, feel the pain, and grieve the loss. There's nothing wrong with doing so. Even a short relationship can really hurt. Next, do *not* make the mistake of trying to push the relationship to the next level, because *a relationship can't be forced*, especially if one of you doesn't want to continue with it. Finally (and I know that this is really, really hard to do), try to see this relationship as an experience that changed you as a person and perhaps helped you learn a little something about yourself. Also, take that intense emotion into a future relationship—with a little luck, you may finally strike gold and move on to the most meaningful type of relationship.

Relationship #4: Long-Term and Deep (Intimate)

If you're really fortunate, you might enjoy a few intimate relationships that last over a lifetime. The people whom I have in this special category are: my wife, my parents and some other family members, and a few friends. These relationships are solid and meaningful, and hopefully they'll last for the rest of our lives. Yet this hasn't always been easy. What separates them from the other relationships is *the reciprocal commitment to share intimate feelings, to work through problems, and to create a lasting bond.*

I'll freely admit that for a long time, I couldn't differentiate a short, intense relationship (Relationship Type #3) from one that truly had a chance of lasting forever. I thought that a few moments of intimacy and sharing meant that the relationship would endure. I'm sure that I even tried to force some of those "summer romances" into a lifetime of love.

I eventually learned my lesson. Instead of placing the emphasis on excitement, I worked on developing a relationship in the right way—slowly and cautiously. I realized that some of my previous partners had different agendas and weren't in it for the long haul. I started to acknowledge that not all Relationship Type #3's would develop into what I'd dreamed of. Sure, I desired a great relationship just as much as the next guy, but the pressure to turn every girl I met into my soulmate lifted.

When you start dating someone, think about the type of relationship it could become. Be prepared for the possibility that you may just make a friend—or you might share an intense passion . . . and never see the person again. But just maybe you'll bask in the glow of a *real* romance and a connection that doesn't end. This is what most of us shoot for, and it *can* happen if we're patient enough and won't settle for anything less.

Dream about the Relationship You Want

First, let's start with a question: If you were in school and had a big midterm or final tomorrow, would you prepare for it? Would you study for that test, or would you not even crack a book? You'd probably make *some* kind of effort to study because you'd care about what happens to you, and you'd be concerned about your grades.

Likewise, if you were looking to purchase a new car in the near future, you'd probably go to the car dealership and speak with the salesmen about the best deal. Wouldn't you also read an automotive magazine or talk with friends about their experiences? Wouldn't you shop around and compare prices? Of course you would, because you'd be investing in something that you'd own for a long time.

A grade in school can affect your future; a car is most likely yours for less than ten years. So, if you take the time and effort to do your homework in these instances—why wouldn't you do the same with a love relationship? I can almost guarantee that you didn't properly prepare for your last one. You didn't take an honest look at the reality of the situation; you just hoped that "things would turn out all right." Yet a relationship is one of the most important areas of your life, so it's puzzling that *an overwhelming percentage of people simply don't do any homework before engaging in one!*

A few years ago, one of my close friends suggested to me, "Why don't you start a series of classes and seminars all over the nation for people who are about to get married or commit to a serious relationship? You could have a weekend deal where they go to classes and answer all sorts of questionnaires. The couples could talk, get to know each other better, and prepare for a great relationship."

As a matter of fact, this idea sounded pretty good on paper—I realized that these people would probably be happier and the divorce rate might go down. But then I wondered just how many couples would actually attend those classes. Do you think that *you* would go? If I came to your town and set up relationship classes, would you be interested? I'd hope that you would, but I fear that most couples wouldn't give this idea a second glance—they wouldn't want to look inside and honestly talk with their significant other about their relationship. The problem is that this kind of class involves hard work, which isn't romantic and usually not too fun or exciting.

It's easier to believe in the fairy tales. It's an enchanting notion—for both men and women—that relationships just "happen." Two people find each other, fall madly in love, and live in blissful happiness for the rest of their lives and never have any problems. However, *this is a fantasy,* and we maintain it because it's not easy to answer the tough questions in a relationship.

So, I've provided a list of questions to help you delve into what your dream relationship consists of. Think of it as "life homework"—research you can do *now* to help you attract your ideal mate in the very near future.

(I suggest that you write your answers down in a notebook—by doing so, you'll spend some time seriously thinking about the questions. You can also refer back to what you've written at a future time, which could be very helpful.)

1. *When you grew up, did you think about your future relationships?*

What did you fantasize about? Of course, all little children have dreams—they may want to become pro athletes, firefighters, or doctors, but this isn't what I'm talking about. The question I'm asking here has to do with what you envisioned for your future. Did you have the all-American dream of living in the suburbs with a white picket fence, a couple of kids, and a two-car garage? Maybe, like many people, you had no idea what form your life would take. This is a critical point, because this fantasy (or lack thereof) plays a major part in your decisions. To make this powerful vision of the future come true, you may have accepted a partner who ultimately can't make you happy, or you might have stayed in an unfulfilling relationship because it's what you were "supposed to do."

For example, let's say that you're a woman who always wanted to be a homemaker and raise a family. There's certainly nothing wrong with that life goal. Anyway, let's assume that you find a man who allows you to do that. But at some point, after the children have grown, you feel like exploring new experiences or want to take a job. Your husband says no, and you give in. Why? To do something different would shatter that old fantasy of being a homemaker. So you stay at home—which is what you thought you really wanted—and you're miserable.

Maybe you're a man who had the idea that he was going to go to work every day and take care of the family. Being the "breadwinner," your intent is to be the sole provider for your wife and children. A lot of men harbor this fantasy because this is what they saw their own father do or because this is what society generally dictates. But instead, you may find a woman who also has a career, so your old fantasy is threatened.

Unfortunately, most of us simply never thought about how our relationships would turn out. We didn't do so because, as a rule, our parents didn't ever take the time to sit down and discuss these issues with us. If you were lucky, maybe you were told about the "birds and the bees," but this discussion probably focused on sex, not relationships. In fact, your parents may have had their own problems and didn't know how to conduct a successful union—even if they wanted to teach you about a good relationship, they couldn't. Perhaps your only example was the poor one they set; consequently, you grew up to follow their pattern or simply had no goals at all.

I find it very sad that schools teach many things that we'll probably never use again (such as trigonometry), but they don't require a course on human behavior. As far as I know, there's no "relationship manual" that's required reading in schools, so children have absolutely no guidance in this area later in life.

The bottom line is that if you didn't have a good relationship to emulate while you were young, or just never thought about what it would take to create an intimate bond, you're already behind in the game. This doesn't mean, however, that it's impossible to catch up. What you need to do now is actively define your ideal relationship and what you want from someone else.

2. What kind of person did you imagine your ideal mate to be?

The typical stereotypes are that every man wants a shapely, blonde, Miss America-type woman; while every woman desires a tall, macho, good-looking guy with all of his hair. Sometimes this is true—there certainly are people who must have the best-looking mate they can find. They won't settle for anything less. There are a lot of different theories that try to explain this phenomenon. Some say that it's genetic—that men and women instinctively want to procreate with the strongest and most desirable member of the opposite sex to ensure genetically sturdy offspring. In other words, to some degree, we're biologically destined to pursue good-looking partners, even if such partners aren't right for us emotionally. This futile search usually leads to a great deal of pain and heartbreak, or a relationship based on superficiality.

Think about this concept for a moment, and see if it's ever happened to you. Take an honest look at your partners, and admit to yourself the real reason you found them so attractive. Was it because of their looks? Or do you have a certain type that you repeatedly go for?

My friend Melissa has had several boyfriends, all of whom could be clones of one another, right down to their height, weight, and hair color. Unfortunately, all of these men have turned out to be very poor partners for her—yet she keeps hoping that the next one will be different. Since she's basing a man's worth on whether or not he's her "type" (fantasy), Melissa is almost programmed to repeat the same scenario over and over again. Other men who don't fall within these narrow appearance parameters don't stand a chance—even though they might share more common interests with her. But Melissa doesn't have a chance either, because her ideal fantasy partner just doesn't exist.

I realize that sometimes it's hard to figure out what characteristics we would really prefer in a life partner. This is because the print and broadcast media generally defines attractiveness *for us*. Adolescent boys and girls are bombarded with images of "beautiful people." The teenage years are critical in terms of self-identity and in defining attractiveness in others, and the media knows it, so what they term *beautiful* somehow becomes the norm. They tell us how our partner should appear, what types of activities they should like to do, and who's "hot" and who's "not." These are powerful messages that cut right to our unconscious, so we may ruin a potentially good relationship because the person doesn't have the "right" look.

This is a shame, as there are very few supermodels—male or female—in the world. The vast majority of people are average looking, but feel inferior when compared to a packaged, preconceived standard of beauty. They spend their lives trying to change the way they (or their partner) look, and consequently miss out on the joy of a real relationship—with a real person.

Take a good, hard look at yourself. Have you gotten caught up in the fantasy that one day you'll find someone who looks just like the models in fashion magazines? I hope that this hasn't happened to you, but if it *has* impacted your choices, then it's time to go in a new direction. Your ideal mate should of course be attractive to *you,* but it's been proven that this isn't the main factor that will keep the relationship strong over the years. So it's time to give up the dream that the ideal partner must be super good-looking, or that you need to stay with someone for appearance's sake.

Right now, spend some time thinking about what other qualities you require from a partner. This exercise is very important, so take some time with it. I want you to specifically exclude any physical characteristics from your list and only focus on *personality* and *character.*

3. What do you require in a partner?

This is a critical exercise, because it compels you to start defining what you *need* from a partner—as opposed to traits that you'd simply like them to have. What are the qualities that you definitely must have in a partner? And are these things present in your current relationship? If not, the next question is crucial.

4. Have you sold out on your dream?

I'll bet that if you think about your friends or family members, you could name a number of them who are in a less-than-great relationship because they sold out and settled for something that wasn't part of their dream. Right now, I challenge you to look at your current partner, or people you've been with in the past. Did you sell out? There's a good chance you did, because a lot of people just sort of sink into a situation that's comfortable. They're neither happy nor really unhappy—they just exist day to day.

But why would someone be satisfied with something that's less that what they desire or deserve? Probably the number-one reason is that they've always placed their partner's desires first. Their own dream takes a back seat, and they go through life trying to please someone else. Their partner's dream becomes their mission in life. A lot of people feel that pursuing their own dream is too self-indulgent, since they were taught to give to others. But *it's truly okay to make your needs known.* A simple change in your language can really make a world of difference, and allow you to get what you want more often. Instead of saying *"He (or she)* likes to go to the movies on Saturdays," try *"I* like to go to the beach on Saturdays." This shift also forces you to take responsibility for how well the relationship is going, as your partner won't be allowed to make all the decisions.

Let's continue to use the word *I*. It's time to take another precaution to ensure that you won't settle for less than you deserve. I understand that it's extremely difficult to exactly define what you need from a relationship, but this next exercise may help.

I want you to write down what it is that you want out of a relationship. Don't think about what you want this very second—determine where you want to be one year from today. For instance, if you're single, do you want to be engaged or married? If you're married, do you want to start a family? If you have a family, do you want to be doing something different from what you're doing right now? In short, *what is your goal in the next year?*

Once this is done, think ahead even further. Apply the exact same exercise to what you want in the *next five years.* This will force you to think on a more long-term basis as far as planning your life and dreams. Obviously, your goals may change. I understand that people alter their plans, often out of necessity or because something better presents itself. So if you do change your mind about the type of relationship you want, then rewrite your goals. This can be done anytime you choose—use this notebook as your own personal life and relationship diary. You *can* develop your own short- and long-term vision of the future.

5. Is your partner a good fit for your dream?

Now that you've defined what you want, can you honestly say that this is what you now have in a partner? I'll admit that this is an extremely difficult question to answer because no one really wants to objectively evaluate their mate's positive and negative qualities. I hope that you've chosen the person who fits perfectly with your personal dream. But it's also all right to be unsure if they're ultimately right for you—it doesn't mean that the relationship is doomed—but it does challenge you to start incorporating your partner into your desires.

Here's a simple example: Let's say that you're the type

of person who realizes that you want to go out to dinner once a week, but you never tell your partner. You justify this by making excuses such as "He's tired" or "He works hard and doesn't want to go out." If spending special time together is really valuable to you, then you need to make this known. So you tell him that you want to go out, and he says no. You then either back down and continue to make excuses, or you push the issue.

But instead, you could tell your partner, "Look, I really want some time alone with just you. We need this to make the relationship survive." By doing so, you're bringing him along into your dream. If you give up, what happens? You'll become angry and resentful and less likely to ask for things you need in the future. So, a wedge will be driven in the relationship—and you're also to blame, because you didn't do your part in making the relationship successful.

> *Relationships succeed not because you've chosen the "perfect" person, but because you work with your partner and honestly communicate your needs to one another.*

If your partner is open to hearing your desires and is at least trying to compromise, then you both have a chance. If they'll never budge, or if they devalue your dreams, then you may have made a mistake in your choice of a life partner. By the same token, if you're not open to hearing and experiencing *their* needs, then it's time to step back and ask why you're unable to compromise.

So your partner must fit into what your personal dream entails. You have permission to make your desires and fantasies the number-one priority in your life. *Define what you need and then stop placing someone else's dream ahead of yours.* What makes their dream more special than yours? Absolutely nothing. Nowhere is there a rule stating that your partner's wishes are more important than yours. This may sound selfish, but the reality is that if you never feel content, then you won't be able to make someone else happy either. You aren't on this planet to just serve someone else's needs. Cherish your partner, but *cherish yourself, too.*

CHAPTER 14

The Honest Relationship

WHY ARE SOME PEOPLE ABLE TO OVERCOME THEIR relationship obstacles, while others are not?

The key to success can't simply be a matter of lifestyle or money—after all, we've seen celebrities, athletes, and leaders of our country engage in self-defeating relationships, when they seemingly had everything going for them. These individuals risk power, status, and wealth because they can't manage to get a handle on their own issues.

Nor can happy unions be predetermined by cultural and background influences—some people from the most modest beginnings have reached the greatest levels of understanding in their lifelong relationships. They rarely argue, co-exist peacefully, and grow into old age satisfied with their life course.

So what *is* the magic secret that those in successful relationships possess? It comes down to an almost embarrassingly simple concept: *Honesty.*

We began our relationship therapy by pointing out the absolute need to look within and define your dream for a relationship. We'll now continue on to the next step, which is the concept of honesty, *with your partner and yourself.* We must do this work now, as the rest of the concepts in this book will only work for you if you're truthful.

It's unfortunate that many times in life we're deluded into accepting dishonest statements. From "I'll call you" after the first date to "I'll never hurt you again" after an extramarital affair, dishonesty destroys the sense of trust between partners. And every time we're lied to, we strengthen that suit of armor we've constructed to ensure that no one will ever get the chance to hurt us again.

But being honest about our *own* feelings and behaviors is challenging because it can be extremely painful. In fact, when I'm with a patient, in the first few sessions I pay more attention to *how* someone relates their life story than to the exact details they give me. This information is sometimes a reflection of how they perceive their life rather than what reality is. The truth will come out, but it's often so unpleasant that the person has to be led kicking and screaming toward it.

So, are you really honest with yourself? I challenge you to *be* honest about whether you *are* honest in expressing your feelings and needs. Like most people in the world, you've probably never sat down and systematically thought about the concept of honesty—what is it, really?

I believe that being honest with yourself means that *you're objective about what you want and where you are in life.* Telling the truth is vitally important, because if you're not able to be frank with yourself, there's little chance that you'll be forthright with others. Unfortunately, most of us are dishonest in some way most of the time—yet without the truth, we're not really free.

Seeing Yourself As You Really Are

At its most basic level, honesty involves *seeing things as they really are.* Many lives have been ruined simply because a person can't (or won't) accept the reality of a particular situation. The truth sometimes hurts, but the alternative is a life built on distortions and lies.

Are you ready and able to take an honest inventory of all the things you've created? Will you make the tough decisions if you find out that you're not satisfied with your partner or life plan? *Can you face your flaws and take action to correct them?* For instance, simply asking the basic question *Am I happy?* can veritably open the floodgates to an honest evaluation of your life decisions.

I hope that you'll make the conscious decision to candidly tell your significant other exactly what you dream about and need to be happy. Keep in mind that *honesty = freedom.* The energy you used to expend covering up mistakes or trying to look good can now be channeled into defining your true self.

But there's one exercise that you must do if you're to have any chance of creating genuine and happy relationships. This involves being brutally honest with the most important person in your life—*you.* Let me preface this by saying that over the years I've treated many patients who simply can't understand why they can't maintain love relationships, friendships, jobs, or family ties. It's fairly easy to identify the main character defect that continues to precipitate these losses—in fact, it forms the basis for most personality disorders: *These individuals don't see themselves as others do.* They maintain a warped vision of their own self-image. For instance, they may feel as if they're loving, caring, and generous—while others see them as selfish, mean-spirited, and annoying. And unless someone actually confronts them on these traits (which seldom happens), these people go through life oblivious to the way they come off to the world. One of my basic goals in therapy is to help my patients almost become objective third-party observers of their own lives.

I give my patients a visual picture to keep in mind—I have them imagine themselves floating above their bodies, looking down at their behavior and words. While still in the process of interacting, I have them observe their actions, and then ask this simple question: *How does the other person see me right now?* That's followed by: *Am I proud of the way I'm handling this situation?* I challenge you to think of these questions several times each day. If you do so, you'll begin to see yourself for who you really are.

Who You Are vs. Who You Appear to Be

It's easy to have a distorted vision of yourself. After all, who wants to admit that they're less-than-perfect? Following are some examples of how to (and how *not* to) see yourself as you really are.

Philip runs a major corporation. Although he's extremely successful, he's also demanding, volatile, and perfectionistic. He'll quickly fire employees in order to save a few dollars on the payroll—viewing this behavior as "just part of the job," because this makes all the shareholders happy. Obviously, Philip isn't a worker's best friend—yet he writes a memo inviting all employees to come into his office for periodic meetings, and encourages them to honestly give him their opinions. If the employees don't take him up on his offer, Philip becomes even more difficult. Deep down, he feels alienated and hurt because he believes that he's a nice guy, and he can't understand why his employees are seemingly afraid of him. Unfortunately, Philip is missing the big picture because he isn't able to see himself as others do. And since no one has the courage to confront him, the cycle continues.

Here's another common scenario. I've spoken to many women over the years who take a certain pride in their ability to remain in unfulfilling relationships, and when asked how an outside observer would perceive their situation, these women usually believe that a third party would find their behavior commendable and a sign of loyalty. Some say that their friends look up to them for "toughing" out an unpleasant situation—but they fail to realize that others actually think that they're weak, dependent, and suffering from low self-esteem. Their psyche protects them from experiencing these feelings, as no one wants to think the worst of themselves.

So, if you were to take a poll of your family members, friends, or former mates, how would they describe you?

Perhaps you don't care what they think, but it's still valuable to know what their opinions are. It would be virtually impossible to talk to *all* of these people, but it's worth reflecting about what they would say (or recalling what they complained about during your relationship).

Here's a tool I use at seminars that usually shocks the participants, but certainly produces results: I ask everyone to envision their own funeral. What do you imagine the attendees would say about you? Would you receive compliments or scorn?

The following is an **exercise** that I'd like you to do with someone who's currently involved in your life. This should be someone who knows you well (such as your partner or a very close friend), but it may be helpful to also choose someone from your public life (such as a co-worker or a friend). You'll probably uncover some sensitive areas, but if you view this exercise as a way to improve your relationships, it's less likely that you'll become angry.

Ask these people, "How do you see me?" You can further expand this topic by asking them to note your positive and negative qualities. Brace yourself, but know that the truth can help you immensely in the future. If you're still friends with a past significant other, it may be useful to ask them this same question.

Now, try to focus on two areas. First, ask: "What are the things I did in the relationship that made it work?" and then, "What are the things I did that caused it to fail?"

Understand that the answers you get may be skewed because of lingering hurt feelings, but nevertheless, you'll probably gain some insight into your behavior. I'll bet that a pattern will develop in which you'll hear about certain negative traits from several sources.

Why is this important? It sets up a path for you to create a great relationship like this one:

Honesty in identifying your poor coping skills ⟶ gives you the chance to correct these flaws ⟶ makes it more possible to have a happy relationship ⟶ allows you the freedom to experience true intimacy ⟶ enables you to express a "true self" to the world.

The Concept of Dishonesty

For all of the positive things that people do in the course of a relationship, there's also one thing they may do that can ruin everything: *They lie.* Most of the time this isn't done on a conscious level—instead, people struggle in frustration, cry with sadness, and claim that they're doing the best they can. But they also cover up pain and lie to themselves. To say that a lot of lying goes on in a love relationship may sound like a harsh statement, but it's not—it's the truth.

What's worse is that lying doesn't even make good intuitive sense, for if someone enters a relationship to better their life, why wouldn't they tell the truth and strive to be as honest as they can?

This is a complex phenomenon, but I believe that the reason for this dishonest behavior is based on one fundamental principle: *In any given relationship situation, people will generally act in a way that minimizes pain and anxiety* so that they don't have to take responsibility for their faults and insecurities.

Here are some of the **forms of dishonesty,** which occur frequently and spoil the chance for growth in relationships. Are any of these familiar to you?

1. Blaming Someone Else for One's Failures

This is probably the most common complaint that I've heard in relationship therapy—that it's "not my fault." Most of the time, the person is genuinely convinced that external forces have wielded insurmountable power over them and can't be overcome. Whether this is seen as making excuses or lying in order to remain a victim, the outcome is usually the same: There's no progress made until the person is able to understand why it's so difficult to be honest. Have they ever had to take responsibility? Were their mistakes always covered up by someone else? Are they afraid of looking foolish after making a misguided decision? Were they always punished, even when they stood up and accepted responsibility for their mistakes? Regardless of the reason, figuring out why someone continually shifts the blame needs to be sorted out, or their relationships will grind to a halt. These people are fooling themselves by disavowing their part in their own actions; consequently, many relationships fail due to this erroneous perception.

2. An Outright Refusal to Analyze Any Type of Failure

Admitting failure definitely causes anxiety, but what's the alternative? Whenever you say, "That's okay. I really didn't want that anyway," you're lying to yourself.

I'm sure you've known someone who always acts as if

they're in control, that any problems they may have are minimal. Or perhaps you've had a partner who downplayed any conflict in the relationship and shut down whenever you attempted to discuss your problems. Those people are being dishonest because they won't see life as it is: Everything is seen through rose-colored glasses, and intimate communication is thwarted in the service of "feeling good."

Over the years, I've had many callers on my radio show say, "One day, out of the blue, he left me," or "She suddenly blew up at me one day." I've given the same response to all of these people: "This didn't just 'suddenly' happen—you chose to not see the inherent problems in the relationship." Some maintain that their relationship is a roaring success, even as their partner walks out of the door for the last time. In the same vein, some people I see in therapy talk superficially about their lives and avoid addressing their real issues. Of course these topics are painful, but tackling them is much more rewarding than just sweeping them under the rug or letting them continue to fester for years.

3. Omitting Key Facts or Details

Dishonesty is also a factor when someone says, "I never told him about it because he never asked me. I never came out and lied to him." This "don't ask, don't tell" policy makes personal growth virtually impossible. Many people have exited relationships when they found out negative things about their partner that were never shared at the outset. Of course, everyone will tell a "little white lie" once in a while to protect feelings or save face, but being consistently dishonest will eventually destroy any chance of a relationship.

Similarly, if someone asks how you're doing and you respond, "I'm fine," ask yourself if you really *are* fine, or if you're just trying to sidestep difficult emotions. If you're avoiding confrontation, this is a form of dishonesty. If you're upset with your partner, *say* you're upset, or you're just cheating yourself out of an opportunity to grow and deepen your bond with another human being.

No Matter What You Call It, It's Still Lying

Let's take a look at a very simple example to prove how easy it is to "stretch the truth."

Henry and Lorna

Henry and Lorna are husband and wife, and they're getting ready to go to a party. Lorna asks, "Honey, do I look fat in this dress?" Suppose you're Henry—how would you respond? If she looks terrific, you breathe a sigh of relief and go right to the compliment. But what if the dress doesn't fit well? What if Lorna's gained some weight recently? Would you be honest with her? Or, in order to avoid hurting her feelings (and continue sleeping in the same bed with her!), would you look her straight in the eye and say, "You look wonderful"?

Henry most likely will run an instantaneous cost/benefit ratio in his head, with the cost being a dishonest statement, and the benefit being the sparing of Lorna's feelings. In this situation, obviously, he decides to fudge things a little in order to avoid an argument. The enlightened man knows that in this case, his wife is *really* asking, "Do you accept me the way I am? Because I don't feel too good about myself today." His dishonesty, even if she senses that he's lying, is accepted and almost embraced as a necessary part of any successful relationship. By stating that she looks lovely, Henry sends the message that he's still in love with his wife, regardless of her flaws.

However, on a more complex level, there's another subtle form of dishonesty being played out in this example. Henry is placed in a tough spot, and he elects to tell a lie. It can be argued that this is a response geared to preserve Lorna's feelings. He's acting in a way that minimizes their collective anxiety and makes Lorna feel good about herself. After all, no one wants to be told that they're overweight and unattractive, so the dishonesty serves a function and somehow seems more palatable. Many people would agree that lying is the right thing to do in this situation . . . or at least it's the lesser of two evils.

The more subtle dishonesty, however, isn't perpetrated by Henry. His untruthfulness is more obvious, but I believe that Lorna is actually doing more harm to herself by initiating this interaction. How can this be? After all, Lorna hasn't actively told a lie to anyone, and she appears to merely be asking for Henry's opinion on her appearance. But suppose she *has* gained a few pounds or selected an unflattering dress? The real challenge for her would be to internally acknowledge this and then go about making a change in her life. She'd be forced into being brutally honest with herself, which, although difficult, could be extremely rewarding in the long run.

Yet this process is avoided because Lorna projects her anxiety on to Henry. She literally puts him in a no-win position. If he lies, she feels good temporarily and is externally validated, but she avoids the tough issue and won't have to make a lifestyle change. If he tells the truth, she may get angry, but the anger will be misdirected outward to Henry when, in fact, Lorna is really angry at herself. She may say something along the lines of "You never compliment me!" or "You always put me down!" An argument will probably ensue, and the deeper issue about her body image is lost.

In either case, Lorna sets things up so that she can avoid being honest with herself. *The real dishonesty is brought about by her reluctance to objectively look inside and see things as they are.* Henry's reaction (the lie) mirrors Lorna's own internal deception. Although it's unlikely that either of them are aware of the damage done to their relationship, they *have* suffered a loss: Henry has lost the freedom to be truthful without devastating another person; and Lorna has lost a chance for introspection and personal growth.

Although almost invisible, the damage is still there. Chances are that the next time Henry and Lorna decide to go out, the same pattern will repeat itself . . . with the same results. The channel of true communication is eroded slowly, but worn away nevertheless.

Another common scenario may further illustrate how dishonesty can impact a relationship and tear two people apart. We'll look in depth at infidelity in the next chapter, but first, let's analyze Tom and Nancy's situation.

Tom and Nancy

One night, Tom, a married man, goes out bar-hopping with some friends. He then returns home to his wife, Nancy, and when she asks how the evening went, Tom states that he'd been working at the office and completely lost track of time. In fact, Tom goes on to tell Nancy that he'll need to stay late at work at least once a week to catch up on "paperwork."

Nancy has no reason to ask her husband if he'd been out with his friends, because he'd been pretty honest in the marriage . . . up to this point. Tom rationalizes that he's following the "no harm, no foul" excuse—no one is injured because Nancy didn't catch him. So he basically forgets about the infraction and goes back to business as usual. He further reasons that since they'd never specifically spoken about whether or not he could go out with his buddies frequently, he "wasn't sure" if this was prohibited. Nancy suspects nothing.

Tom is relieved that he doesn't have to tell an outright lie, since Nancy never actually comes out and asks the critical question. In fact, he rarely thinks about the consequences of these evenings and goes on to steadily increase his time away from home. The next thing Tom and Nancy know, they're in divorce court. Nancy is devastated by Tom's indiscretions, and when asked why he didn't tell her of his activities sooner, he replies, "I didn't want to hurt you."

Do you feel as if Tom should have told Nancy the truth long ago? Before we answer that question, it's worth noting that nearly everyone who gets away with unacceptable behavior will hide it—either by a lie of omission or by denying that anything happened.

Who would approach his wife and proudly state, "Well, dear, I want you to know that I was dishonest with you this evening. I wasn't at work—I played poker and drank all night and left you home alone. I hope that you'll forgive me"? Hardly anyone would have the courage to say this, for a variety of reasons.

But on a deeper level, Tom is probably ashamed of his actions, and he's frightened that he'll be caught. It can be strongly stated that Nancy deserves to hear the truth from Tom—even if it leads to pain and anger. Maybe she wouldn't even have been upset to know that Tom needed some time with his friends once in a while! But Nancy shouldn't have to find out on her own, or be the last to know. Ideally, when one person in a relationship does something wrong, they tell their partner—then they work things out or go their separate ways.

But it's not an ideal world—Tom doesn't confess to Nancy, and so the other part of this story unfolds. I believe that the real tragedy here is Tom's refusal to be honest with himself. After the very first sign of sneakiness, he should have taken a serious look at his own behavior and tried to understand why he felt the need to cover it up. Tom's thinking shouldn't have centered exclusively on whether to tell his wife or not—he should have tried to understand the forces that drove the betrayal. That's the critical mistake here, and what eventually led to the marriage's dissolution. *Tom simply wasn't honest with himself,* and so—by being unwilling to acknowledge why he wanted to spend time away from Nancy, in addition to the obvious lies he told her to cover up the nights out—his deception was two-fold. Tom then became trapped in a downward spiral, as he piled lie upon lie.

Dishonesty then became the new way of living in Tom and Nancy's marriage, because on some level, he had to maintain the fantasy that his actions weren't really hurting Nancy or their relationship. Once Tom was able to get away with the behavior just one time, the significance of this was disavowed and he easily began to "live a lie."

As you can see, the phenomenon of dishonesty feeds back on to itself, as it becomes necessary to lie about the importance of the lies in the first place! The truth is buried and lives are destroyed.

Why We're Dishonest

After examining the previous two cases, it could be assumed that lying is done on a conscious level, meaning that people are aware of the reasons for their dishonesty. It may surprise you, but this is usually not the case. Excepting for sociopaths (who maliciously lie for personal gain), most of the time dishonesty in a relationship comes courtesy of decent people who are genuinely trying their best to live a happy life. But on an intellectual level, almost everyone can see that being dishonest leads to negative outcomes and knows that lying is a dysfunctional coping skill.

Defined in another way though, *dishonesty in a relationship is best viewed as a defense against an unacceptable emotion.* This is a key distinction and something that I stress in therapy. If it's the wrong thing to do, then there must be a powerful force that drives people to lie. Dishonesty can produce anxiety in and of itself, but it must also lessen the distress associated with another emotional state that's more unacceptable. One anxiety is traded for another, with lying representing only the symptom of the underlying struggle.

This process can be represented in this way:

> The avoidance of an unacceptable emotion
> or relationship discussion ⟶ leads to
> dishonesty and lying to a partner ⟶ but
> also leads to evading a greater anxiety.

For example, in the case above in which Tom went out with his friends behind Nancy's back, it probably caused less internal discomfort for him to lie to her than to have to negotiate a compromise about being "out with the boys." The key for Tom would have been to acknowledge his fears about telling Nancy—and then to address this issue. Had he done so, the outcome of their marriage could have been quite different.

We're all dishonest with ourselves at times; it's easy to recognize the blatant lies we sometimes tell. Once in a while, we suffer the consequences and try to pick up the pieces. And if we're lucky, we don't lose marriages, jobs, and friends in the process.

The other form of dishonesty is much more subtle, and much more difficult to change—therefore, it's potentially much more destructive to a relationship. This is defined as a *failure to see things as they are.* Denying reality, in any life situation, represents a lie to yourself. You may wonder, *Why is it so necessary to be absolutely truthful to oneself all of the time?* After all, some of the greatest achievements are made possible by a spirited pursuit of dreams that fly in the face of reality. But some have had the motto that "The sky's the limit!" . . . only to come crashing down to earth because they didn't envision the obstacles and realities of life.

Merely hoping for a good outcome doesn't assure success in the end. People *hope* that their partner will someday change, *hope* that they'll somehow dig themselves out of a financial hole, *hope* that they'll live a long life after smoking for 40 years . . . it's easier to live in a world of dreams instead of accepting the limitations of life.

Dishonesty ultimately serves the function of guarding against two difficult feelings: hopelessness and disappointment. We don't like to experience these emotions, but avoiding them in the short term ironically sets the stage for bigger disappointments later on! We pay the price on down the road for closing our eyes to what's really happening now.

Being Dishonest about the Real You

I can almost guarantee that you haven't always been "on the level" with your partner, and you don't even recognize the extent of what you're doing. When you entered a dating relationship in the past, you were probably dishonest at times, although not in ways that were conscious. You probably didn't intentionally *try* to deceive someone else, but you did something very common on the first few dates. For instance, you most likely didn't share that you still live with your parents or have a job that only pays minimum wage—after all, no one really shows their true colors at first. So by that same token, you're probably not going to find out that your boyfriend is being sued for evading child support or your girlfriend was sexually abused. These are things you tend not to learn about someone until way down the line. The reasons for this are usually: "I didn't want to leave a bad impression," or "I didn't want to scare off my date."

For instance, I've had several callers on my show claim, "I met this wonderful person."

I usually ask, "How long have you known each other?"

Sometimes the answer is surprising: "Well, about a month or two, and we're going to get married!"

This immediately raises a big red flag to me, and I issue the challenge, "What do you *really* know about this person?"

The caller customarily protests, "I've been told everything. He's been open about the past. I know all about his family, about what he wants in life. . . ."

At this point—because it's my job to be the reality tester—I'll usually issue a strong warning. I understand that it's easy to miss things when you're in love and you desperately want to believe that the person is everything they represent on the surface. But the caller is taking a risk by naively thinking that there's nothing else to be learned about this person whom they're about to embark upon a lifetime commitment with. *Failing to acknowledge that people leave out the "not-so-good" stuff early in a relationship is being dishonest with yourself.* Very vew people intend to *actively* deceive or hurt someone that they're dating, but it is deceit nonetheless.

We simply don't want to share potentially embarrassing details about ourselves during the first stages of a relationship—this is expected, and probably won't cause your relationship to end. The reluctance to accept the fact that someone you're dating is probably not being 100 percent truthful with you leads to a false idealization and hope that can only be called a type of dishonesty. The resulting disillusionment impacts your future as a couple.

When I point out these facts to callers, they'll sometimes retort, "I was kind of scared to talk about my feelings. I've heard that if I genuinely say how I feel, he'll be turned off."

I point out that this is another form of dishonesty, as it doesn't give the other person the chance to make an informed decision on continuing to date the "real" you. They see a façade—which someday will crumble. Why not save a lot of time and energy up front and just show who you are at the beginning of the relationship? That way, there are no surprises down the road, and no one feels betrayed.

The *unsuccessful* relationship scenario unfolds in this way:

> By trying to "look good" ⟶ you hide insecurities and real feelings ⟶ which promotes a false image of yourself ⟶ establishing a relationship grounded in dishonesty ⟶ which angers your partner as your true characteristics emerge ⟶ resulting in a significant danger of losing the relationship.

The same algorithm applies if you're the victim of a partner who isn't initially truthful. The stage is subtly set very early in the dating process, with huge ramifications resulting—even years later. Two people seeing only what they want to see causes major problems, as each realizes that they've been duped.

Holding in Your Emotions

I understand that it's difficult to know exactly when to reveal honest emotions, for your partner is then given the power to hurt you. This is never more evident than at a point in the relationship most of us have experienced: telling a partner that we love them for the first time. *When do we honestly acknowledge our feelings and tell somebody that we're in love with them?* Nothing is as painful as when one partner sheepishly whispers, "I love you" for the first time . . . only to be met with silence and a stunned look. If the sentiments aren't reciprocated, the dynamic of the relationship is forever changed—usually for the worse.

Women feel as if the man will run away because he thinks this means immediate marriage, and men sometimes have a hard enough time just choking out the words, since they've learned that it's not "manly" to express feelings.

So when *is* the absolute right time? It's got to be when it feels right for you. Sure, if you love someone and then verbalize it, they might say to you, "I don't love you back." That hurts, but at least you know the reality. You may not accept this, but you *know,* and it all started with an honest statement.

On the other hand, if you play the waiting game, there will be a tradeoff. Let's say that you hold it in—you want to express your love, but you're scared. You choose to simply hope that you're loved in return, but you're afraid to really find out, so you disregard your feelings (a form of dishonesty) and say nothing. What will happen next in the relationship? Things may move along for a while, but eventually, you'll become resentful because you could never say how you felt. It may not be a conscious resentment, but the anger *will* come out.

Many people hold in emotions because they fear that they won't get the response they desire in return. They base their honesty on whether the other person will listen and say what they need to hear. Someone I knew actually said, "What's the use of being honest if nothing good comes of it?"

A perfect example of this occurs frequently in dysfunctional families. A lot of times, families aren't honest with each other. Buried "secrets" and hidden agendas make it impossible for family members to fully express themselves without fear of retribution. They end up in my office years later with a string of failed relationships because they never learned how to be honest. Mom and Dad lie to each other, the children are promised things that they never receive, and real expressions of feelings are discouraged in order to give the appearance that everything's all right. A lot of people grow into adulthood having had to disassociate anger or resentment that wasn't tolerated by insecure parents. But as adults, they don't have the courage to confront those responsible for these feelings, so they're mentally trapped.

Consequently, the feelings they've never faced seep out into their love relationships, or they end up shutting down when they need to speak up the most. I've asked several patients why it's so difficult to confront their parents on the past, and most don't understand the reason. They'll say, "I'm scared," or "It's too late," or "I moved on. It's over now." I then try to convince them that it *does* matter. Parents aren't gods, and they make mistakes—just like anyone else.

The important message is this: *Telling people how they made you feel is one of the most freeing experiences you can ever hope to attain.* Developing this skill alone can make you better at constructing successful relationships later in life.

How to Be Honest

Honesty, therefore, is an inherent part of the relationship therapy presented in this book. And know that it *is* possible to become more honest with yourself and others— it's certainly not easy, but it is absolutely necessary in order to have a mature, open relationship. Honesty flows from a feeling or thought inside of you. You then:

Recognize the feeling and attempt to own it. Know that it's okay to feel a variety of strong emotions. We're humans, not robots. We *all* feel anger, jealousy, happiness, sadness, pride, and depression—among other things—as a part of living. Even if you were told at some point in your life that it wasn't okay to experience these things, they can't be submerged forever. Successful people don't hold their emotions inside; instead, they utilize productive coping skills to manage their effects. Try to understand where your emotions come from, but even if you don't, let them be present. Embrace this as a chance to feel alive, and celebrate that you're being honest about who you are.

Make a plan of how you'll express this feeling to the person to whom it's directed. When you're in the heat of battle, it's usually not the proper time to adequately process the emotion. Many people make this mistake— they yell and scream at each other and assume that the problem is solved, when in fact nothing of substance was accomplished. If it will help, write down the things you absolutely need to say. It's easy to forget important aspects of an issue when trying to deal with painful emotions.

Tell the person your feelings. It doesn't matter if they initially don't respond to you in a positive manner— you've done it! Of course it helps if they're receptive, but this may not be the case. I believe that you've opened the door for a stronger bond in the relationship, or found out that you can't be accepted for who you are. Either way, you now know where the relationship stands, and you can act accordingly.

There's no good reason why you can't commit to being honest with yourself and your partner. You also have every right to expect that this approach to your relationship will be reciprocated. If it's not—that is, if your significant other has the habit of withholding feelings and thoughts, or blatantly lies about their actions—then your relationship is in big trouble. You'd be lying to yourself if you thought otherwise.

Perhaps stretching the truth at times won't completely ruin your chance of having a great relationship. But there *is* one form of dishonesty that will be sure to change your relationship dynamic forever. This is so prevalent that I've devoted an entire chapter to it.

Lying in your love relationship is serious enough—but this next phenomenon I'm about to discuss is much larger, because it makes the *entire relationship a lie*. The ultimate form of relationship dishonesty is coming up next.

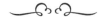

CHAPTER 15

How to Handle Infidelity

A N INTIMATE CONNECTION THAT WILL STAND THE TEST of time must be based on *trust*—otherwise you have a relationship built upon dishonesty. If you find yourself wondering when your partner will betray you next, then your relationship is in serious trouble of ending. A great relationship should be a two-way street filled with openness and commitment, instead of a one-sided affair where you're the victim.

This brings us to the topic of this chapter. *Infidelity* jumped into the center of our national news recently courtesy of former president Bill Clinton, who cheated on his wife but claimed he hadn't. His actions are certainly not unprecedented, though—celebrities seem to be unfaithful to their spouses on a regular basis yet act as if nothing untoward has happened. On a smaller scale, each day thousands of average people see their relationships completely decimated when their significant other embarks on an affair with someone outside of their marriage.

It seems as if infidelity has become an epidemic—one with serious consequences in terms of this country's escalating divorce rate, the increasing number of children born out of wedlock, the spread of sexually transmitted diseases, and the massive personal devastation visited upon a person who finds out that their partner has had intimate relations with someone else.

We'll spend the rest of this chapter discussing how infidelity affects relationships. It truly is the *ultimate relationship betrayal,* because the entire foundation that a relationship is built on becomes a lie.

You may be breathing a sigh of relief, thinking that you can skip this chapter because you've never been cheated on or had a relationship end due to infidelity. Well, the following statistics may jolt you back into reality: Recent research has found that approximately 35 to 40 percent of married men will have a sexual encounter with someone other than their wives. This high rate validates many women's opinions of men and their propensity to stray—unfortunately, it was also cited that approximately 25 percent of all married women also commit infidelity. Do you think that on the day they pledged lifetime faithfulness to each other, these future adulterers were thinking, *Until death do us part . . . or until either one of us finds someone who is a little better or sexier?* I highly doubt it.

So what goes so terribly wrong? Is it that all people who cheat are inherently dishonest and uncaring? Or is it that generally decent folks find themselves unable to resist the temptation to embark on a new and exciting sexual escapade? Common sense is obviously thrown out the window, since many smart people who should know better get caught up in the moment and risk their marriages, families, and friends for a night of passion.

As one caller to my radio show said to me, "I just got swept away with emotion. I couldn't stop myself. I lost everything."

Defining Infidelity in Your Relationship

I heard a very interesting definition of infidelity once from an acquaintance of mine named Jerry. He reasoned that he was cheating only if he actually had *sex* with a woman other than his fiancée, Felicia. Kissing, "petting," and oral sex weren't cheating for him—since there was no sexual intercourse. When I asked him what Felicia would think of this creative rationalization, Jack said (to my surprise), "I don't know. We've never talked about it. She's never asked me, and I'm certainly not going to tell her." So Jack went on to have several intimate sexual moments (but without intercourse!) with other women during his engagement to Felicia, and he felt completely at ease.

Would you agree with the reasoning behind Jack's behavior? I couldn't imagine that Felicia would have been okay with marrying him if she knew that he'd been with other women behind her back—no matter whether they went "all the way" or not.

The problem here occurred way before Jack made the decision to be with other women. Perhaps this outcome could have been avoided if he and Felicia had sat down and defined what each of them considered to be acceptable behavior. Felicia's mistake was assuming that her definition of infidelity matched Jack's, when in fact, they couldn't have been further apart.

The lesson for you to learn here is that *you must talk with your partner about what is acceptable to do with others, and what is not.* You must discuss these things *early* in your relationship. I understand that it's not romantic, and no one wants to have this conversation, but there's no substitute for a dialogue about the *limits* you expect one another to meet. Don't assume that you both have the same standards, especially when it comes to a universal definition of infidelity.

I'm assuming, of course, that you've actually thought about the subject of cheating at all. If you haven't done so, I suggest that this is the time—right now—to consider what infidelity means to you. What behavior would you absolutely not tolerate from your significant other? To help you get started with this exercise, I'll illustrate several examples that you should think about carefully and then talk about with your partner. If anything, this will make for a lively interaction and help your relationship immensely!

Which of these situations do you define as infidelity?

Situation #1: Your partner has sexual intercourse with another person, but just once. Is this an example of infidelity? The vast majority of people would agree that this is blatant unfaithfulness.

Situation #2: You find out that your partner has been carrying on an affair for several months. Is this cheating? Again, I can't think of many people who would overlook or excuse this behavior.

Situation #3: Your partner engaged in oral sex or other forms of sexual contact *(but didn't have actual intercourse)* with someone other than you. In your mind, is this cheating? Believe it or not, some people (and apparently Bill Clinton) would say that this isn't a form of infidelity.

Situation #4: Your partner has never had any physical contact with a "friend" of the opposite sex, but spends a lot of time with this person sharing intimate life details. Your partner and his/her close friend also go out together a couple of times a week. Is this tolerable to you? Is this a form of cheating? Can infidelity take on the form of emotional betrayal?

Situation #5: You find a stash of pornographic magazines or discover that your partner has been visiting "adults-only" Websites or going to topless bars. Have you been cheated on? Do you consider the act of viewing naked strangers for pleasure an act of infidelity?

Situation #6: You find out that your spouse has been frequenting bars without wearing their wedding ring. A friend tells you that your partner hasn't been caught doing anything physical with other people, but there's been a lot of flirting. Is your spouse being unfaithful to you?

Situation #7: Your sex life has dwindled, yet you catch your partner masturbating. There's an admission that this has been going on several times a week when you're not around. Do you feel cheated on?

I'm sure that you haven't thought about these situations in any systematic way, yet these are the behaviors that destroy countless relationships, so it's not too soon to define what you can or can't tolerate in your relationship. Perhaps you'd be okay with any of the scenarios listed above, or maybe you think they're all unacceptable. It's not up to me to tell you what will impact your relationship—*it's your responsibility to define what you think is infidelity, and then communicate this to your significant other.* After all, your definition of cheating may be very different from mine—or your partner's.

With that said, I feel compelled to offer up what I believe is a reasonable definition of cheating. I first heard this from Karen Hand, co-host of my radio show, and it seems to encompass a variety of concerns:

Infidelity (cheating, betrayal):
You're engaged in a behavior of a sexual or intimate nature that you cannot openly discuss with your partner.

I believe that this way of thinking about cheating is brilliant, because it encompasses several important concepts. There are two parts to the process of cheating—the act itself, and then the concealment and the lies—and the definition above includes both parts that contribute to the betrayal. Inherent in this definition is also the idea that the honest partner is getting "cheated out" of something valuable in the relationship—such as open communication, commitment, and the belief that they won't be used or hurt. This definition also shows that infidelity can include nonphysical factors. You can be intimate with another person . . . without even touching them.

This definition simply states that *you* should be the number-one person in the world with whom your partner shares fears, hopes, dreams, disappointments, and love and sexuality. Your partner shouldn't have any secrets about *anything* they do when you're not present—because when you're getting "cheated on," you're also getting "cheated out" of a relationship based on trust and honesty.

So firm up your beliefs about infidelity, and you'll minimize the chance that you'll ever hear your partner declare, "I'm sorry. I didn't think you'd care if I was with someone else."

Why You or Your Partner Would Cheat

The news shoots through you like a knife. Your partner, whom you've trusted unconditionally, has confessed to being with someone else. You get angry, sob hysterically, and feel as if your whole world has been turned upside-down. You've been betrayed in a big way and don't know where to go from here.

Then you remember that one of the main goals in any relationship is to *understand* each other's behaviors and motivations. After you calm down, your *first* task is to *determine why infidelity has entered your life*. There can be no substitute for this process if you're to stand any chance of picking up the pieces after such a serious betrayal. (This also holds true if you're the one who strayed). Later in the chapter, we'll talk about whether you should even try to stay with a partner who has cheated, but either way, you should seek to understand why this happened in your relationship. What could have caused this treachery?

Sexual Reasons

The most obvious factor contributing to infidelity is a *sexual* need. This is undoubtedly where you'll focus most of your energy if you've been cheated on. I've heard many people ask, "What has that other woman (or man) got that I don't have? Isn't *our* sex life any good?" This is usually the first area that a hurt partner will look to for answers, because it seems to make sense that most people will cheat for purely sexual reasons.

Of course, sex may well be the reason your partner has strayed. Someone else looked good, the adrenaline started to flow, and there was no turning back—before they knew it, a moment of attraction had turned into a night of sexual passion, with no regard for potential consequences. Your partner's mind, which had been protesting, "Don't do it!" was vetoed by an overwhelmingly pleasurable physical feeling in their body.

However, common sense dictates that if sex is satisfying for both you and your partner, then the risk of infidelity is greatly minimized. Sure, there will always be those people who can never get enough, regardless of how great the sex is in their primary relationship, but this isn't the norm. If you do have satisfying sex in the relationship and your partner (or you) still can't resist the temptation to cheat, then it's time to reevaluate the commitment.

If you hear the excuse, "But it was only sex!" this may be true. The goal from here, if you decide to attempt a reconciliation, is to *take a hard look at your own sex life and honestly identify any shortcomings or points of dissatisfaction.* If you can get beyond hearing the details of the affair (and this is a big if), then it may be worthwhile to talk about what you and your partner really want from each other sexually so that these behaviors can be considered as ways to pleasure each other in the future.

I've known couples who have survived an episode of cheating in the relationship and then went on to have even better sex because they felt free to verbalize exactly what they liked. Unfortunately, this doesn't happen too often, as the image of your loved one having intercourse with another person is so powerful that many couples simply can't come together sexually again. The damage is just too painful and difficult to overcome, so any semblance of a healthy, mutually enjoyable sex life is lost.

Emotional Reasons

The mistake that many people make is to assume that infidelity is all about an unfulfilled sexual need. Of course, the behavior is sexual, but the psychology behind it must also be based in emotional factors, and these reasons simply can't be overlooked. Don't be naïve and assume that it's just about the sex, because, in a lot of cases, it's much more than that.

Emotional factors can sometimes be more important than physical gratification. People also cheat because they're getting something emotionally from, or are able to achieve a level of intimacy with, another person that isn't possible with their partner. Sometimes it's an *escape* from the arguments and conflicts at home that ruin communication and that special feeling partners have for each other. Cheating is clean and easy, without the fighting and bad feelings. A cheater can define the affair as something "good," as opposed to their committed relationship, which has been "tainted" by years of difficulties. The affair is like a new start—without strings attached.

At other times, people use an affair as a viable outlet for feelings of *anger* and *resentment* toward their partner. This is the passive-aggressive approach, as the cheater won't verbalize any angry thoughts, but instead performs an act that will hurt their partner. They're able to release all of their pent-up anger and "get back" at their mate— all in one fell swoop. Many times, the unfaithful party isn't even consciously aware of this motive.

After years of a stagnating relationship, a sense of *boredom* can also set in. But instead of looking for new ways to generate passion *within* the relationship, the cheater looks for a new person—outside the relationship—to provide excitement. This is the easy way out. Instead of talking with their partner about the missing spark, the cheater will go out and attempt to create a new one. Relationships can feel smothering at times, and to avoid that "trapped" feeling, the cheater will set out to unconsciously prove that they're still "free" or have "still got it."

In all of these emotional factors, the bottom line is that, by having an affair, the cheater is getting some psychological relief from an unpleasant situation at home. But whether they get to feel "wanted" again, are working out some anger issues, or have set out to prove their desirability—the solution is the same.

Both partners must be willing to sit down and discuss these emotions in an open and honest way. The unfaithful party should allow their partner to verbalize their sense of betrayal and grief over the affair, and the person they cheated on ought to be willing to understand the emotions that led them to stray in the first place. This is tremendously difficult relationship work, and it usually takes actual face-to-face therapy with a counselor.

Unresolved Issues from the Past

We all have past experiences that drive our current behaviors—being unfaithful to a partner is no different. You should consider the possibility that you or your partner may be *replaying a dynamic from the past.*

Was there a pattern of cheating between important figures in your past (such as your parents)? Was keeping secrets a part of the childhood experience? Did you get used to keeping family secrets, or did you always feel left out of the loop? Did either of you see significant people in your lives lied to, betrayed, or hurt? And finally (and this is a critical question to answer), have you ever been unfaithful in previous love relationships? Better yet, have you ever been faithful to *anyone?*

If you've been cheated on, it's quite possible that your partner needed to set up a dynamic with you in which you'd be hurt emotionally, just as they were wounded by important people in their past. Again, reasons within this realm probably require a serious attempt at therapy with a trained counselor, or else your relationship is most likely over.

Your Partner Sees You As a Doormat

If there's a pattern of infidelity in your relationship, make no mistake about it—*you* must share some of the blame! Your partner may have cheated on you because you *allowed* the behavior to happen. It's understandable that you may not have seen the first episode of infidelity coming, but after that, it's fair game. By this I certainly don't mean to imply that cheating is acceptable, but you'd better be aware that there's a good chance it will happen again—even if your partner says they're sorry and pledges complete faithfulness.

A lot of great people get cheated on simply because they don't put a stop to it. They naively believe empty promises, and are then startled when the dishonest behavior continues. I once counseled a woman named Helen who continued to take back her husband after he'd cheated with multiple other women for years. Helen's rationale was that her husband would eventually "come around" and see what a wonderful person she was. Unfortunately, she shared him with his mistress on many holidays, exposed herself to sexually transmitted diseases, and watched as her family got torn apart. I told Helen that this was as much her fault as his—but she didn't like my way of thinking, and didn't return to me for therapy anymore. She's probably still suffering through a terrible marriage, but she gets to maintain the belief that she's a martyr for sticking it out.

The reality is this: *As long as you allow this behavior to continue, your partner will probably continue to cheat on you.* How do I know this? Much research has supported the fact that after a single episode of cheating, the odds rise that you'll be cheated on again. This doesn't mean that your relationship is necessarily doomed, but there is a *lot* of hard work for you and your partner to do if anything is to be salvaged. It's natural to hear what we want to hear and hope for the best after a significant betrayal, but also keep in mind that your partner may do whatever they're allowed to get away with until you put a stop to the cycle of dishonesty.

Think about it this way—if your relationship is your partner's top priority, then there would be no cheating, because they'd never want to do anything to hurt you. If your vows of commitment had any meaning at all, then there wouldn't be any unfaithfulness. If you made it clear that *any* type of infidelity would be met with serious repercussions, then I'll bet your partner would think twice before stepping out with someone else.

You'll minimize the chance of being walked over by your partner if you do the following:

- **Make it known that infidelity will not be tolerated.**

- **Watch out for red flags that indicate you're being cheated on,** such as changes in your partner's dress or in their sexual behavior toward you; a pattern of spending more and more time away from home "working" or going out; or an emotional distancing/decrease in communication as evidenced by evasive answers or difficulty telling you the details of their day.

- **Do your homework and find out if your partner has cheated on other people in the past.** By the same token, if you cheated with

your partner while they were in a previous
relationship, what makes you think that
they won't turn around and do the same
thing to you?

The Other Woman (or Man)

I would be remiss if I didn't mention another destructive
form of infidelity: You're the *third party*, cheating with
someone who's committed to someone else. I could have
placed this material under the "doormat" heading above
because this is most likely the way you're going to end up
feeling. I can't state strongly enough that you should *not*
become involved, sexually or romantically, with a person
who's married, engaged, or in a committed relationship—
even if they're begging you to have a liaison with them.
You're taking a huge chance that you will end up devastated
and alone.

One of the most pathetic examples of this that I have
ever heard of came from Theresa, a woman who called my
radio show one evening. She'd been carrying on an affair
with a married man for several years, but he hadn't left his
wife because the "timing wasn't right"—it was always the
kids, his job, or his fear of hurting his wife that got in the
way of his committing fully to Theresa. So year after year,
Theresa hung on, consoling herself with the unfounded
belief that this man would be all hers one day. She never
pursued any relationships with available men that might
actually have had a real chance of succeeding. And then
one day, the man Theresa had been having the affair with
did leave his wife—and moved in with a woman whom
he'd been cheating on Theresa with!

The moral of this story is that *one way or another, you'll get burned in the process of cheating.* If you're the one cheating, you'll be found out someday and may possibly lose everything that you value in your life. If you're the victim of an unfaithful partner, your relationship will never be the same. But if you're the "other" person on the side, you'll only be forming a partial relationship and will have to share your love interest with at least one other person. No matter how you could rationalize any of these behaviors, the result will only be heartbreak and pain.

Can a Relationship Be Saved After Infidelity?

One of the most common questions I'm asked goes something like this: "My partner cheated on me. Where do we go from here?"

I usually assume that they're hoping that the relationship can somehow be saved and things will go back to normal. I shatter this illusion very quickly when I tell them that *their relationship has been irreversibly changed, and nothing will ever be the same.* The relationship as they knew it is over, and a different one is now beginning.

Their next question is predictable: "How can I trust my partner again?"

My answer is always the same: "I don't know of any quick and easy way to regain a sense of security and trust in someone who's brought another person into your intimate relationship without your permission. What are you going to do the next time your partner goes out with friends or shows up at home a little late? What will you do when you find an unfamiliar phone number or hear an unrecognizable voice on the telephone asking for your partner? What will you be thinking of the next time you and your partner try to have sex together?"

These are incredibly difficult problems that taken alone could end the relationship. There's no way around it—the aftermath of infidelity is set up to be a cycle of suspicion and mistrust. You may never recover enough to feel comfortable with your partner ever again.

But if there's any desire or chance to save your relationship, you should honestly answer the following questions. Hopefully these will guide you in the right direction and make your ultimate decision clearer.

1. Is this the first time infidelity has been a factor in the relationship?

Has your partner cheated before? Have *you* been unfaithful? Is this a recurring pattern in the relationship? My feeling on the frequency of cheating is a "two strikes and you're out" theory. If your partner makes a mistake once, but vows to never do it again, at least there's a fighting chance to save your relationship.

But if you can't tolerate one incident of cheating, then be quite honest with yourself and set your sights on ending the relationship. After the first betrayal, you have every right to leave your partner, even if he or she is pleading to be forgiven. If you attempt to continue the relationship and then there's a second affair (or even a one-night stand), then you really are playing with fire by sticking around for more. The pattern has been established, and you'll just continue to lose self-respect and dignity.

2. Should you stay together for the children's sake?

On this one, my opinion is that you need to size up in your mind what's better—letting your children see Mom and Dad go through marital problems, or allowing them to learn the lesson that no one should tolerate a partner who betrays the other parent? I know that both of these solutions have major drawbacks, but this is your choice— you're going to have to pick one or the other, unless both you and your partner lie to your children and try to act as if nothing has happened. But remember that kids are very perceptive and usually know more about what's going on in their home than you think they do.

My feeling is that both Mom and Dad can still be parents to their children, even if they don't live together. So my answer to this question is no, you shouldn't stay together just for your kids. But don't put them into the middle of the marital issues either. That would be completely unfair and selfish.

3. Is the cheater willing to completely give up their affair?

It would only make sense for your partner to drop the affair after it's discovered. Yet, unbelievably, some people will bargain with their partner, attempting to continue to see the other person from time to time. If you're to stand any chance at all of putting the infidelity behind you both, *the affair must end*. Period.

Actually, this shouldn't even be a question. It should be a demand that your partner will *never* again see that other person. If there's a refusal to accede to this ultimatum, then it's time to pack your bags and move on.

4. Has the unfaithful partner agreed
to see a relationship therapist?

It's a very fortuitous sign when your significant other volunteers to go to therapy to understand why they had the need to commit infidelity. However, when there's resistance to getting help, or an attitude of "we'll figure it out on our own," it doesn't bode well for the relationship.

Here are the words you want to hear after an affair: "I'll do whatever it takes to save this relationship. I will never see the other person again, and I'll go to counseling. I'll commit to making our union the top priority in my life, no matter how long it takes."

If you don't sense this spirit of renewed commitment, it's going to be an uphill battle to make the relationship work again, and it may not be worth your trouble.

5. Are you still in love with the person
who cheated on you?

Sometimes you can get so caught up in the specifics of the affair and how to recover the relationship that you forget to ask yourself this fundamental question: *Is there any love left, or am I so angry and resentful that no amount of therapy will make the relationship whole again?*

I tell my patients that they may never be able to recapture a loving feeling, and that it's better to admit this than to try to force the relationship in that direction. Some people fall out of love immediately when they've been betrayed. Recognize if you're in this category, and then act accordingly.

6. Most important, is there any joy left in your relationship?

Does the pain that you feel outweigh the joy that's left for you both? Do you still have any common interests and goals? Or was the infidelity just a symptom of a relationship gone bad long ago? How much happiness did you experience in the relationship before your partner was unfaithful?

I can only hope that you and your mate will consider the tremendous pain and complications that an affair causes. If you're ever tempted to become intimate with someone else (without your partner's knowledge), visualize this picture: Imagine your significant other breaking down and hysterically crying in pain, all because you chose to inflict such agony and humiliation on them.

Is this the way you deserve to be treated, or the way you should treat another human being? Just remember the tremendous upheaval infidelity leaves in its wake. Yes, it *is* possible to overcome this betrayal, but only time, love, and hard work can ever heal this wound. Is being unfaithful worth all of these consequences?

CHAPTER 16

Relationships That Can Destroy Your Life

SOME MISGUIDED (AS FAR AS I'M CONCERNED) RELATIONSHIP experts insist that, even in the worst of times, you should stick with an unfulfilling relationship and find ways to make it work. And if you can't make it work, then you need to figure out what's wrong with *you*.

I'm familiar with the implication that we take vows "for better or worse" and shouldn't give up on relationships too easily. There's certainly nothing wrong with the concept of commitment and loyalty in a marriage or long-term union—it's the cornerstone of success. After all, I wrote this book to assist you in finding ways to cope with your relationship obstacles and to help you improve your chances of keeping your partnership alive.

But the fundamental problem with the "hang in there, no matter what" theory is easy to pinpoint: *Maybe, just maybe, you made a mistake* at the very beginning and simply chose a partner who is causing you great misery and pain. Given the high divorce rate in our country, many people have obviously come to this conclusion. Perhaps they're more in tune with relationship dynamics than most "experts" are.

Of course I believe that you ought to give your relationship your all and shouldn't just bail out at the first sign of discomfort. The point I'm making here is this: No matter how hard you try, and no matter how much effort you exert to change the dynamics of a relationship, if you choose the wrong partner—that is, someone who has destructive relationship tendencies—then the relationship will never reach its full potential and you'll be very unhappy.

Did You Make a Mistake?

So why is conventional wisdom so wrong when it comes to relationship debacles? Maybe it's not politically correct to admit that you've made a mistake that needs to be corrected—after all, certain religions view divorce as taboo and demand that you stay married, no matter what. What expert wants to be known as the guy who says that some relationship problems aren't fixable, and that certain relationships just shouldn't continue?

So, I'm taking a risk here by taking a stance that's sure to be unpopular. I maintain that sometimes two particular individuals simply don't belong together—never did and never will. There may be nothing fundamentally wrong with either person in the relationship, but our society says that if you just "heal yourself," the relationship will somehow improve dramatically. The fact is this: *Sometimes two people are able to find happiness apart, but they bring out the worst in each other when they're together.*

The real problem you're facing may have been set in motion long ago. For a variety of reasons (discussed later), you simply made a wrong choice in a partner. Perhaps you found someone who wasn't great relationship material, or maybe they lacked that one vital ingredient you require for a lasting union. You and your partner just aren't compatible enough for things to work out well. This doesn't mean that individually you're both doomed to fail; it just means that as a couple, things don't mesh.

There's no way around the fact that you and your partner have to coexist on a daily basis. A satisfying relationship is made up of two people who *want* to be with one another continually, and for it to work, common sense says that there has to be a level of shared interests and compatibility between the two.

I have great respect for Dr. Phil McGraw and his message on relationships. He has certainly put forth some outstanding ideas in his books and on the *Oprah* show. He's generated a fresh approach to solving relationship problems. I find that I agree with most of what he says, and we share a similar "tell-it-like-it-is" style. We differ on one point, though: Dr. Phil claims that it's a myth to believe that a happy union requires common interests that bond you together forever. He also says that a relationship *can* survive with a flawed partner—maintaining that if you work on yourself enough, your partner will come around and your relationship will thrive.

After dealing with many people struggling with difficult relationships, I've come to the opposite conclusion: *Compatibility is an essential feature of a relationship destined for greatness.* For instance, I'll bet that if you went out and asked several couples who have been together for many years, "What has kept you in love with each other?" you'd probably see the same themes repeating themselves over and over, such as common interests, a delight in being together, shared beliefs, cultural similarities, and compatible goals. These are the people who have chosen the right partner. The real myth should be that opposites attract and stay together—sure, there may be an initial lust, but over time, partners who aren't somewhat similar to each other won't remain together.

In addition, there are some individuals with so many unresolved issues that it's nearly impossible for them to carry on an intimate and committed relationship with you. It's entirely possible that your partner *is* too flawed for a relationship—and no matter how much time and effort you devote to helping them, it will never result in anything positive or beneficial.

So let's spend the rest of this chapter looking at the types of relationships and partners that you should probably steer clear of, since they could be destructive to your life.

The Partner Who Won't Acknowledge a Problem

You may have chosen the wrong partner if they're unwilling to critically look at the relationship. I list this first because this is without a doubt the character trait that will destroy a relationship the quickest. It seems incredible that someone would see their relationship collapsing around them and yet refuse to acknowledge a problem or seek professional help, but believe me, I see it happening all the time.

The end result is almost always the same—the relationship is over or one partner just gives up and lives with the pain. Sometimes it's the woman who won't get help, but more often than not, it's the man. After all, a whole industry has been built around techniques to get a man to open up about his feelings and problems, and sometimes this is successful. But I've heard the same complaints a hundred times: "He just won't admit there's a problem and won't talk to anyone,"or "He tells me that I'm too needy and shouldn't feel this way."

If your partner refuses to seriously analyze significant issues and conflicts, then it should be a bright-red warning flag that you'll probably never be on the same page regarding growth in the relationship. I know that a lot of people are wary about going to therapy and think that it's a waste of time, but once in a while, you reach an impasse that can only be solved in counseling. Furthermore, if you both disagree on the following basic relationship issues and don't get some help, there will undoubtedly be trouble ahead:

- **Children**—whether to have any and how to raise them.

- **Money**—who will earn it and how to spend it.

- **Fidelity**—what it means; that is, how far can you go in your interactions with other people while still respecting your partner's wishes?

- **Power**—how much do you have when reaching important relationship decisions? Does one of you take charge even if the other disagrees?

- **Your basic living situation**—where to live and how to respect each other's space.

There's certainly no shame in admitting a problem, and your odds improve if you both get some help during the difficult times. But if an issue arises that threatens to be a relationship "ender" and your partner won't seek outside help, you're up a creek without a paddle, so to speak.

The Addict

Your relationship may be destroyed if either you or your partner has an addiction that isn't being addressed. I know that this is a controversial area, because many people with various addictions go on to create long-lasting marriages. But most addicts aren't successful at relationships, primarily because they haven't made the commitment to become healthy—for their partners *or themselves.*

When someone is dependent on *anything,* it automatically assumes great importance in their life. I'd hope that your partner is addicted to making you happy and causing the relationship to flourish, but sometimes this is just not the case. For a variety of reasons (biological and psychological), some people are so involved in addictive behaviors that they can't put in the effort to make the relationship a priority.

I'm sure that the first thing that comes to mind is the all-too-common scenario in which someone is involved with an alcoholic. Millions of people drink alcohol on a regular basis, and millions fight alcoholism. Whether you view this as a disease or a psychological weakness, the result is generally the same. Alcoholics (who haven't gone through treatment or who haven't stopped drinking completely) won't be able to give what it takes to create a lasting relationship. Why is this the case?

The answer is simple: They're so involved with the addictive cycle that they become uninvolved with *you*. Any interactions you may actually have will probably be upsetting, since they'll tend to focus on how much your partner is drinking, how irrational they may be, or your pleas for them to get help. Since the relationship revolves around the addiction, the intimacy and the friendship get lost in the shuffle.

You may be saying to yourself, "Well, this doesn't apply to me. I'm not married to an alcoholic." So let's expand the definition a bit further: *An addiction is something that someone needs in their life on a regular basis, no matter the cost to themselves or others.* The behavior is repeated over and over, even in the face of significant consequences. When we think of it this way, the possibilities expand greatly. Here is a list of addictions (the major ones come first):

- **Drug use and dependency** (similar to alcoholism, described above).

- **Gambling** and/or frivolous spending of money.

- **Pornographic materials** (including books, magazines, films, cable TV, the frequenting of strip clubs, solicitation of prostitutes).

- **Large amounts of time spent with others to the exclusion of the partner.** This also includes the "workaholics" who regularly ignore their families and partners.

- Repeated episodes of **infidelity,** including Internet relationships.

I understand that there have been many books devoted to the above subjects, so my point is not to exhaustively discuss every permutation of these areas. I'll be happy if you just recognize that addictive behaviors are going to be destructive to your relationship. Of course it can be argued that many people occasionally use drugs, spend too much money, bring pornography into their sex lives, work too much, or cheat on their partner—all without ruining their relationships forever.

The critical distinction here is the *amount of time and energy invested in a particular pursuit, to the exclusion of the partner.* This also takes into account that the addictive behavior is something that you're not willing to tolerate in the relationship. If you're okay with your partner constantly ignoring you and potentially self-destructing, then this will obviously not apply to you. Believe it or not, I know of some people who just don't care what their partner does away from the relationship. I also know of some relationships in which *both* people are addicts, and they somehow find a way to coexist. This is pretty rare, though, and usually they've got other major problems to deal with in life.

But I assume that you, like most people, won't be happy unless you have your partner's attention and respect—which is certainly your due. The bottom line is this: *Whatever the repetitive behavior, if you ask your partner to make the effort to stop it and they disregard your request, the relationship is in huge trouble.* If they continue to ingest addictive substances, cheat, throw away all of the money, or make their friends/work their top priority, then you have to face the fact that you're number two (at least), not number one, in your partner's life. You've ended up with a partner who values other things more than you. So, do you want to walk around constantly feeling angry and resentful, or do you want to spend your life with a partner who makes your *happiness* their addiction?

The Abusive Partner

Let me make one thing perfectly clear: *You're absolutely in a destructive relationship if your partner abuses you.*

Over the years, I've been called into a number of emergency rooms to see acute psychiatric cases, and many times I've been faced with a woman who's a mass of bruises and broken bones after being battered by her significant other. What's amazing to me is that in nearly *all* of these situations, the woman will receive medical treatment—and then refuse any psychiatric intervention. It's heartbreaking to see her drive off with the man who inflicted the battery on her, because I can almost guarantee that she'll end up right back in that emergency room, courtesy of someone who "loves" her. The saddest part is that, yes, she has physical wounds, but I can guarantee you that underneath, there are much deeper scars on her soul.

It seems maddeningly obvious that no one should ever stay with a partner who dishes out physical, verbal, or emotional abuse. Yet every day there are millions of people who can't break away from an abusive partner, and thus suffer repeated blows to their self-esteem. Maybe the relationship didn't start out that way (it almost never does), but soon a pattern of dangerous interactions develops, in which one or both people get hurt.

When I've asked victims of abuse why they would stay in a destructive relationship and tolerate such mistreatment, the answer is invariably, "Because I thought I did something wrong and deserved it." They've been led to believe that *they* are the evil one in the relationship, and that they're actually the *cause* of their partner's angry outbursts. Usually their abuser has claimed that he or she wouldn't have had to inflict the pain if they weren't "made" to do so by the victim.

Well, here's a message to anyone who's involved with a partner who says or does debasing and degrading things, including frequent name-calling, put-downs, yelling, screaming, hitting, or any other action designed to lower one's self-esteem. Believe this, because it's absolutely true: *They're the one with the problem, not you!*

Yes, this is a relationship problem that you both have to face, but the abuser's lack of control over their anger is the real concern that needs to be addressed. You need to accept the reality that your partner has serious psychological issues that need to be sorted out, and unless they get some immediate professional help, you're most likely condemned to a relationship full of conflict and pain. Your life could very well be destroyed—so know that this is *not* the right match for you.

Finally, I'd like to say one more thing on this subject. Usually I feel as if I'm talking to a brick wall when I attempt to counsel someone to move away from an abusive partner. I've heard the following hundreds of times: "He hits me, but I love him. I'm the only one who understands him."

While I realize that we'll sometimes go to any length to hang on to the belief that our choice in a partner was a good one, this can lead to a syndrome of minimizing and justifying their outbursts. You also need to understand that someone who exhibits a pattern of recurrent abusive behavior will most likely *not* change. What impetus is there to change if you're all too willing to quickly forgive and forget? If you're living through a nightmare of physical or verbal abuse, *I implore you to take the steps to end this cycle by getting out* while you still have some self-respect to recover.

The Partner with Significant Unresolved Childhood Issues

Some of the most successful people in the world have overcome terrible childhoods. We've all seen the inspiring stories on TV of people who overcame great odds and went on to attain their goals. A lot of these folks had virtually no model for good parenting and guidance while growing up, yet they managed to rise above their obstacles. It's easy to just think of these people as products of the inner city, or of poverty-stricken families. Yet, I'm here to tell you that some of the most damaged people in this world didn't come from the places you would expect. What I've learned over the years is that you simply can't judge someone's stability by how many advantages they enjoyed as a child.

Big homes, expensive clothes, great wealth, and a high-powered job won't be enough to ensure that someone is good relationship material.

Tara and Dean

Tara, a patient of mine, had been seriously dating Dean, a guy from one of the area's most prominent families. He'd grown up in a beautiful home, with parents who were pillars of the community, and after breezing through college, Dean was now an heir to his family's empire. Tara almost couldn't believe that she'd landed what appeared to be the catch of a lifetime—Dean had chosen *her* over the dozens of other women he'd been seeing. She was enamored of him, and in her mind, he could do no wrong.

The only problem was that Dean *did* do a lot of things wrong. Sure, he was handsome, charming, intelligent, and savvy in business, making millions of dollars for his company (along with a rather substantial sum for himself). But over time, what emerged was a portrait of a man who simply did not have what it took to hold together a personal relationship. Dean ignored Tara for long periods of time, dated other women on the side, and was incapable of engaging in meaningful dialogue about her feelings. As Dean went through life accumulating more and more possessions, Tara became just another object to own. Yet she hung in there, hoping that Dean would change for the better. "After all," she said to me during one session, "he had such a normal childhood. I can't figure it out."

What Tara didn't understand was that, in fact, she really had no idea what kind of childhood Dean had experienced. She made an assumption (a faulty one) that what his family had displayed in public was indicative of what went on behind the closed doors of their mansion. Tara didn't understand the following principle: *Some of the most significant psychological damage done to someone during their childhood is due to things not so readily apparent to an outsider.* For instance, many people weren't obviously abused during their formative years, but they still bear character flaws that destroy any chance of their having a great relationship. Tara found out the hard way that just because Dean's façade was extremely attractive, inside he wasn't what she was looking for at all. If she'd done a little bit of digging into his childhood, she might have saved herself quite a bit of heartbreak down the road.

Childhood issues will be extensively discussed later on, but one of these two core dynamics is always at their root:

1. **You (or your partner) got *too much* of something** as a child, either positive or negative. Controlling or overindulgent caregivers, abusive parents, or an overstimulating environment all fall into this category.

2. **You (or your partner)** *didn't get enough* **of something** that was vital and necessary as a child. In the above example, Dean simply didn't receive enough attention and unconditional love from his parents, who were usually out in the community impressing others or making more money. He was left to fend for himself, and suffered a massive amount of abandonment and rejection. These unresolved issues played out in all of Dean's adult relationships.

The ultimate truth about childhood issues is this—*you won't be able to quickly tell what baggage your partner comes with from the past, but it will manifest itself at some point.* For your sake, I hope that this baggage won't significantly interfere with the relationship, but if there *are* family conflicts that persist into adulthood, you may be in for a rocky road in your relationship.

Naturally, there are many people who get the proper counseling and put their past behind them and form new and improved coping skills—they have a fighting chance at a relationship that lasts. But many more go from one unfulfilling relationship to the next because they play out childhood dynamics that they've never understood. (As a footnote, Dean has now been married several times and is currently going through another devastating divorce, yet he's still out wooing naive women—who can't possibly imagine the difficulties that await them.)

There's only one way I know of to minimize the chance that you'll end up with someone who's permanently scarred from childhood events: *You must ask questions about their past and learn something about their upbringing.*

If they refuse to discuss it, watch out. If the answers include sexual abuse, abandonment by parental death or divorce, adherence to rigid beliefs or rules, or estrangement from parents or siblings, then watch out. Things could get rough for you in the relationship.

Now this doesn't automatically mean that your fate is sealed. If the other person is open to getting help and treats you with respect, consider giving a relationship with them a go. If they insist that there's nothing wrong at all, then you need to be aware that you may be heading down the destructive-relationship road.

The Partner with Dysfunctional Past Relationships

You may have chosen the wrong partner if they have a pattern of relationship fiascos. Now, there aren't many people in the world who haven't had at least one relationship end on a disagreeable note, or found themselves in a situation that just didn't work out, but once in a while, you end up with someone who's left behind a trail of broken hearts. Everything goes along swimmingly with this person initially, as they wine, dine, and romance you, leading you to believe that the relationship will progress further. Then something terrible happens: The phone calls stop, the flowers stop arriving, and your partner is suddenly "busy" most of the time.

You're sent reeling, desperate to learn why the relationship went sour. You hadn't done anything different, but something drastically changed for the worse. You're jilted without reason, and you feel rejected by this person. So you start calling and writing them to find out why you were "dumped," and you never get a response. You're left hanging, but you decide to move on to a new relationship. The problem is that you're still preoccupied with wondering how you managed to screw up the last time. You feel as if you must have done *something* wrong, so you take considerable pains to figure out what that was.

Unfortunately for you, this is a huge waste of energy. A better use of your time would have been to do your homework about your partner *in the beginning*. By learning about their past relationships up front, you could have possibly foreseen what was in store for the two of you. I've argued with many colleagues over this point, but I believe that it's grandiose of you to think that your relationship will turn out differently if your partner has engaged in a string of relationships that follow the same dysfunctional pattern. *What your partner has done in past relationships will be what he or she tends to do with you!*

Rationalizing that "we're different; that won't happen to me," is a naive attitude that could bring you much pain. I hope that things *are* different for you, but don't bet on it. You must become informed early on and learn as much as you can about your partner and their past relationships. Then you'll know what to expect, and be able to identify the problem areas before you get to the point of no return. While this may not be ideal conversation for a first or second date, you've got to ask the questions sometime! Here are a few questions that could help you assess your partner's relationship potential:

- Do they understand what went wrong in their past relationships? If they always **blame other people,** realize that this may be a person who won't take responsibility for failure.

- Is there a **pattern of cheating,** or overlapping relationships?

- Have they ever spent time alone? People who **quickly go from one relationship to the next** may have issues with dependence or abandonment.

- Have they just ended a serious relationship (it doesn't matter why)? If so, your chance of making this a committed relationship is diminished. As a rule, **rebounds** don't work.

- Is there any pattern of **abuse** directed at previous partners? I realize that they probably won't come out and proudly announce, "I used to hit my wife!" but there are ways to find this out, usually through their friends and family members.

- Do they now **"hate" their ex** due to a volatile divorce or relationship breakup?

- Have they been a **serial dater,** going out with many people but never forming more serious relationships?

Obviously, there are many people who have failed relationships and subsequently go on to find the love of a lifetime. So I'm not saying that if any of these issues is a factor you should immediately start running—but be aware of the red flags. If you choose to be with someone who has many divorces under their belt, or has a pattern of short-lived relationships, realize that you're taking a chance. If you're a gambler, go ahead and roll the dice. Just be informed about the odds against creating a successful connection with someone if their past relationships haven't turned out so well.

The Loveless Relationship

You may be in a destructive relationship if you or your partner is emotionally or sexually shut down. Many authors have coined catchy phrases to describe this character issue. I've heard terms such as "someone who just can't love," the "ice queen," and my all-time favorite, the "commitaphobe." Regardless of the moniker, the fact is that some people aren't capable of opening up enough to make a relationship last—if this is the case, you probably chose the wrong partner.

So why would someone enter a relationship but then close down emotionally or sexually? One possible reason could be that they've simply never learned how an intimate relationship progresses. They may not have the skill to really let someone else into their inner world, or they may be afraid to let anyone get close to them. After all, there's a distinct amount of vulnerability inherent in sharing feelings and fears. Opening up means that you give your partner the power to either accept or reject you. This is tremendously difficult for some people, and they'll go to great lengths to avoid feeling exposed. Ironically, their efforts to maintain control and avoid conflict in the relationship usually leads to their ultimate rejection. They close down to avoid being hurt . . . but then feel great pain when the relationship ends.

Allison and Richard

A woman I know named Allison used to like "bad boys"—guys who were exciting, yet were unpredictable and seemed ready to explode at any minute. Allison finally figured out that these guys would never be good marriage material, so she wound up with Richard, a man she described as "nice and boring." Allison thought her troubles were over because she and Richard never fought, he would do whatever she wished without argument, and they had common goals. . . . They were divorced less than two years later.

What on earth could have happened? Well, Allison found out that although Richard certainly was a nice guy, he could not tolerate any type of emotion in the relationship. When Allison attempted to verbalize her feelings and needs, he wouldn't even listen or respond. They had little in the way of a sex life, and when Allison would tell Richard that she was angry, he'd usually give her the "silent treatment," sometimes for days. He refused to seek psychological help, claiming that the marriage was fine, when in fact, it was falling apart. Allison really didn't have a relationship at all—she felt as if she were living alone. Stereotypically, men have more difficulty sharing feelings—but this was way off the chart.

Another group that characteristically has significant problems opening up emotionally in a relationship are the serial daters. You want them to settle down with you, but they can't; they're always out searching for other dates. Even if they do make a commitment to you, their door is always open in case something "better" comes along. You never feel as if you have *all* of your partner, and constantly worry about the possibility that they're going to stray. This pattern may keep you coming back for more, as if you need to prove that you *can* get them to finally open up. Then one day, they just leave—without a hint of sadness—and you wonder how they could be so callous. The answer is simple: *You never had them in the first place because they never let you inside!* You chose an unavailable partner.

So what does it mean when someone *is* emotionally available to you? I'm certainly not suggesting that every single issue in your relationship has to be rehashed over and over or that you and your partner need to have gut-wrenching discussions on a regular basis. But I *am* saying that your partner should at least listen to you and participate in a dialogue about the relationship. You should have a partner who shows you some physical affection, both in private and in front of others. You should have the feeling that if you weren't around, it would *matter* to your partner and they'd feel like something crucial was missing. A good mate will share what they're thinking and feeling with you because you're a priority in their life.

The Explosive Relationship

At the other end of the spectrum from the Loveless Relationship is the Explosive Relationship, which is what you have when it seems that you and your partner can't go a day without arguing or clashing in some way. Of course there are times during any love relationship when you'll both disagree and get angry. But then, with calm heads prevailing, you'll sit down and work together to find a reasonable solution. The key here is that you work *with each other as a team,* and you don't let things get personal.

Some couples that I've known, however, are unable to have a relationship based on mutual respect and courtesy, and *almost every interaction they have has the potential to erupt into a full-blown fight, either verbally or physically.* It's amazing to me how often these people stay together, as they exhibit considerable contempt and bitterness toward each other. When they're in the same room, frightening things start to happen—yelling, insulting, object throwing, and humiliation seem to be the name of the game. It's extremely embarrassing and painful to watch couples like this in action.

I used to think, *If they could only see themselves being so mean and ugly to each other, then surely they'd put an end to this behavior.* Then I realized that the cycle is self-perpetuating—the more they fight, the more they *want* to fight, in order to regain the upper hand. They can't see that maybe they simply don't belong together, since all they do is play on each other's deepest insecurities, jealousies, and character flaws. There's no love or mutual support going on here.

Why would you choose to stay in a relationship filled with constant anger and degradation? If you don't think that a relationship can exist any other way—well, you're wrong. The happiest people I know work *with* their partner in a spirit of admiration and love, without putting the other person down or pouncing on their mistakes or shortcomings.

Just ponder this for a moment: *You lose a little bit of yourself each time you or your partner is allowed to say something hurtful or insulting.* You may not realize it, but a chunk of your self-esteem is taken away, and little by little, you lose a sense of what's positive about your relationship, since you're *both* behaving in shameless ways.

There's not an easy solution to this type of relationship. Your options are:

- to continue on a path of vindictiveness and anger, with the goal of completely destroying your partner's psyche;

- to make an unbreakable pact that you'll only use positive and constructive language; or

- to end the relationship in order to preserve any dignity that you both may still possess.

I certainly wouldn't want to spend the rest of my life in a relationship filled with rage, nor would I want my sensitive spots exploited by a partner who seized the opportunity to hurt my feelings every chance they got. I'd realize that there's someone out there who'd want to bring out my best, and who'd want to grow old with me.

In this chapter, we've defined what type of relationship or person could be destructive, and how to determine if you've chosen the wrong partner. We'll uncover the reasons *why* you've been attracted to certain types of people later on. There are complex motivations that underlie your choice of a lifetime mate—so it's absolutely essential to understand why you love and lust after particular individuals.

But right now, let's find out what it takes for a man or woman to be a *healthy* partner. This is an extremely complicated issue, as it takes a little bit of luck and timing to connect with someone on the deepest of levels. Just because your partner has some shortcomings doesn't mean that the relationship won't work. It's fairly easy to identify obvious flaws that should make you think twice, but much more difficult to know exactly what those flaws will end up meaning for you in particular. After all, even psychics can't predict the future with 100 percent accuracy.

My feeling is that there can be a million different qualities that will make a relationship work, but there are certain essential character traits that must be present. What are they? We've already identified some of them in the form of the Relationship Contract (see page 9). I think it's important that you go back now and reread the conditions that form this contract. If you and your partner are abiding by these principles, you're off to a great start. If not, it's not over yet . . . but you've got some work to do.

Let's move on to identify some of the essential ingredients necessary for a love relationship that *will* work for you.

CHAPTER 17

The Relationship That Will Survive

I T SHOULD NOW BE OBVIOUS THAT SOMETIMES THERE'S A fine line between a union that lasts and one that will eventually fail. Occasionally, two mature, well-adjusted people get together but don't succeed at their relationship, while conversely, two people with major issues can stay together for years. Is it just a matter of luck that any relationship works out at all? It's true that every once in a while, you'll find a couple who can feed off of each other's afflictions, with their relationship stumbling along yet never breaking apart—but by no stretch of the imagination can this be called a healthy relationship.

Since we've spent the last two chapters identifying relationships that probably won't work for you, let's shift gears and look at *aspects of a successful relationship*. At this point, I'm going to make the assumption that you've already formed a solid foundation with a stable partner. But don't rest on your laurels just yet—there's still some work to be done.

What Is a Healthy Relationship?

I believe that there are certain things that must exist in a relationship for it to last a lifetime. Before I reveal these qualities, let's start with an **exercise** designed to help you look at relationships in depth. Although this may seem simplistic, I hope that you'll put some thought into it.

On a piece of paper, make two columns. The first column should have the heading: *A Healthy Relationship.* Here, you'll list all of the qualities that have made your past and present relationships satisfying, such as things that you or a partner did that strengthened your bond with each other. What do you think are the absolute essentials that must be present for any love relationship to go forward and succeed?

The next column should be titled: *An Unhealthy Relationship.* Write down any of the behaviors or qualities you or your partner have exhibited that ruined previous unions—really put some thought into the habits that tend to destroy your relationships.

Of course, most relationships fall somewhere in between these categories, but using extreme words may help your define your lists. For instance, start thinking about the qualities that constitute a really positive, healthy union. Is there anyone in your life (such as your parents, siblings, or friends) who you think have a really out-standing relationship? If so, list the things that they do to make the relationship work. What attributes do they have—separately and together—that ensure success?

Now think about a really unhealthy relationship you've witnessed. Maybe you have a friend who got divorced or your parents split up. This could also be an opportunity to look at one of your own unsuccessful relationships. What happened?

Here's an example.

A Healthy Relationship	An Unhealthy Relationship
Couple puts each other first	Couple is immature and jealous
Couple loves each other above all else	Couple cheats on each other and lies
Couple shares similar goals and interests	Each partner tries to control the other's behavior

I'd like you to do this exercise so you can start systematically analyzing your relationships, just as a therapist would do in his or her office. In fact, all the exercises in this book are ones I actually use with couples who are having trouble, or for individuals who haven't been able to form long-lasting relationships.

Invariably, though, there are certain qualities that *don't* show up in these exercises—yet the five characteristics below are among the most important items that I use in my *own* definition of a "healthy relationship."

I refer to these character traits as the "Five C's" of a great relationship. Really think about whether you've ever experienced problems with these areas in a current or past love relationship.

The First C—Consistency

Consistency means that your partner does things in a certain pattern that's *predictable* over time. One consistent objection to this point that I've heard is that this usually leads to boredom in the relationship, since it's no fun to know what your partner will do day after day.

But what's the alternative? You don't want to be on the relationship roller coaster for the rest of your life, never having a clue as to how your partner is going to interact in certain situations (see Chapter 5). It may seem exciting and mysterious when your mate does something impulsive that catches you off guard. Of course some spontaneity can light some fire under a relationship, such as when you shake up your daily routine or surprise your partner with a thoughtful gift, but this isn't the unpredictability I'm referring to.

Instead, I'm talking about the way you get treated emotionally and physically over time. *Consistency leads to security and peace of mind, which are both paramount in successful relationships.* Inconsistency leads to fear, and the anxiety of "what's going to happen next?" This results in a power struggle. Inconsistent people usually can't hold relationships together over long periods of time.

For instance, maybe you've been in a relationship where your partner's anger was inconsistent. One thing will set off their temper; the next day, they're unruffled by the very same thing. When they walk in the door each night, you can't predict their mood, so you walk on eggshells to prevent conflicts. You've given them the power to make you act in a certain way. You simply never know what's coming next, and there seems to be no rhyme or reason to your partner's moods.

Many women in abusive relationships find themselves stuck in this pattern: As her husband is beating her up, he'll say, "But I love you!" This simply doesn't make any sense logically because his behavior and words aren't consistent. Someone doesn't beat up his wife if he truly loves her.

Yet, in a lot of cases, the woman stays because she hears the magical "I love you." It's extremely tempting to remain in this relationship because, after they make up, the husband will usually say that he'll change and is really sorry. His behavior is inconsistent, but he plays to the woman's notion that things will someday get better.

Some people even feed on inconsistency because there's an excitement in never knowing when their partner will be home, who they've been with, if they're lying, or if they'll be in a bad mood. These relationships will fail because this unpredictability can only produce anxiety and helplessness in the long run.

Therefore, you must be able to count on consistency from your partner in the following situations:

- Dealing with problems

- Responding to certain difficult situations

- Handling their temper

- Not cheating on or abusing you

There's only one situation I know of in which consistency can be detrimental to a relationship: This is when a partner consistently does *nothing* for the relationship! They never send cards or flowers, share their intimate feelings, say that they love you, give you their undivided attention, or make you a priority—the list could go on, but it's obvious that these are consistent counterproductive behaviors. *Overall, though, someone must have the ability to consistently treat you in a loving and respectful manner.* If they don't, you both will be quite unhappy.

The Second C—Commitment

The motto *commitment to excellence* is often bandied about in sports circles. A similar promise is sometimes used by major corporations, as they proclaim that they've committed to excellence by serving the public and making the best products they can. But commitment is also crucial in individual relationships.

Sometimes this word is overused, but to me, *commitment* means that someone has taken a vow to stay in the relationship even during challenging times. People who don't take this word seriously will flee a relationship when things get tough.

To be sure, commitment isn't always fun. It requires patience, and the ability to look ahead and realize that things usually get better after you've weathered the storm. A lot of people who aren't successful in life relationships lack this one fundamental trait—they commit themselves only when things are wonderful, but make excuses and discard the relationship when difficulties arise.

A critical distinction must be made now between *commitment* and *comfort*. Your partner (or you) may stay in an unsatisfying relationship simply because it's easy and familiar, yet they'll never actively work to make the relationship better.

There have been hundreds of times when I've instructed someone to get couples counseling with their partner. Most of the time, they'll reply that it's impossible because their mate refuses to go, customarily saying that they can solve their problems "on their own" without the help of a therapist. Men are usually more resistant than women to getting therapy, even if they recognize that there's an issue. So, the woman will usually drop the discussion, and the relationship will continue to unravel. She'll make the excuse, "But he says that he loves me and wants to try to work it out." Sure, he wants to work it out, but only on *his* terms!

So, commitment isn't just about staying put. After all, anyone can sit around the house and not communicate—that's not difficult to do. *True commitment means that your partner actively works to solve problems in the relationship, and treats you well in the process.* The relationship is the number-one priority in their life. They commit to not hurting you; they don't cheat; they don't lie; they don't say hurtful things to you. Above all, they commit to letting you grow as a person and don't try to control your behavior or hold you back. If these qualities are present in your love relationship, then it has a great possibility of surviving.

Finally, your partner should also commit to being consistent. If they say that they'll be home by 7 o'clock, then they should try to be home by then. If this isn't possible, then they need to make a phone call, since they've vowed to be courteous to you. If, for example, your husband says that he'll take the children to the park on Saturday, then he needs to do it. If actions consistently match one's words, the relationship is on the right track. But if you're not getting this from your relationship, or you notice that *you* have a pattern of not committing, then it's time to reevaluate this very important concept.

The Third C—Caring

The obvious question that you must answer honestly is "Does my partner *care* about me?" Most likely, you'll answer with a yes. Even if the relationship is terrible, most people will say, "But he told me he loved me," or they'll maintain that their partner really did care about the way they felt.

But consider this definition of *caring* and see if it matches what you're experiencing in the relationship: *Caring implies that your beliefs and feelings are on an equal par with your partner's.* You don't necessarily have to agree, but you respect and value each other's opinions. *Your partner cares about your personal growth.*

It's easy to confuse caring with *control*. Control is *not* one of the C's. In a controlling relationship, all major life decisions—including which car you'll drive, which job you'll take, and how many children you'll have—are made by your partner, ostensibly because they "care" about you. This dynamic happens frequently in relationships, and initially it can feel good that someone else "cares" so much that they'll take on all of the responsibilities. But is this really caring? Or is it a form of narcissistic control, designed to covertly take away the threat that you'll grow on your own?

A caring person allows their partner to grow in life. If there's a setback, the caring person is there to console and support their partner. Caring means to *give up* control. *A caring partner consults with you on life decisions and wants to understand your feelings.* Dinner and flowers every Friday night is great, but this alone doesn't show a true commitment to caring. It takes much more than that to enrich both individuals' lives in the relationship.

The Fourth C—Compatibility

I know that we discussed the idea of compatibility in the last chapter. I'm not trying to be redundant by bringing it up again, but I want to stress the importance of this concept. If you and your partner aren't naturally compatible, then the relationship is bound to have some rough patches that may be too difficult to overcome.

I've heard the argument many times that opposites attract, and this may be true. There's a powerful initial attraction, but over time, opposites also tend to *detract* from each other. *Your relationship will be much easier to manage if you're able to find someone else who shares your goals, values, and interests in life.* I mean, it's hard enough to find anyone in this world with whom you can really connect on a deeper level, so don't make it more difficult on yourself and choose someone with completely different beliefs from you.

Before I go any further, I know that there are some of you reading this right now who think I'm crazy. After all, you've been able to create a great relationship with a partner of a different race, religion, or culture. I commend you for this, because it shows that some couples *can* get beyond huge differences. I'm not trying to imply that different styles of living can't be integrated into a cohesive relationship.

The point I'm trying to make is that you and your partner need to be headed in the same direction. I've seen countless couples break up because they simply couldn't agree on basic goals for their relationship; or on matters related to children, finances, or logistics (such as how much time to spend together and where to live). For example, if you're the type of person who needs a lot of time with your partner, and they're always on the road, will this be ultimately satisfying for you? If you wholeheartedly want a family but your partner absolutely does not, then how do you make a decision that satisfies you both? If you hold strict religious beliefs and your partner holds opposing views that are just as strong, who will win out?

I just want you to think about this concept very carefully: *A healthy relationship isn't about one partner winning or losing, or having to give up cherished values.* If there's a winner or loser, then you both miss out in the long run. Whoever has to give in usually feels resentful and envious, and whoever emerges victorious feels guilty.

I'm often asked to pinpoint the best way for a single person to meet someone who could be great relationship material. There are literally hundreds of approaches, but only one will dramatically increase your odds of succeeding: *Live your life by pursuing activities that genuinely interest you.* Don't go to bars if you're not comfortable there. Don't buy a dog just to strike up a conversation in the local park. Don't place yourself in a situation that you dislike just because you hope to meet someone. Believe me, it's easy to spot those who are obviously scoping out the crowd and looking desperate.

This way of living will only assure that you'll meet incompatible people.

I don't care what you enjoy the most—by following *your* passion with energy and enthusiasm, you'll be in a position to meet others who share the same goals. You'll probably come to find that these individuals are compatible with you. At least you've got common ground to start a friendly conversation. Remember—even couples who have been married for 60 years had to have something that bonded them together from the first moment they met.

The Fifth C—Compromise

I played a lot of team sports when I was younger, so the concept of cooperation was drilled into my head at an early age. I remember all too well how selfishness can ruin the game: Once, one of my teammates completely went against everything our coach had instructed us to do and went his own way—the whole team collapsed, and naturally, we lost the game. We all got a sore reminder that day that in a team sport, you only win by working together. It's a hackneyed phrase, but there's no "I" in the word "team."

By committing to a relationship, you've just formed your own two-person team. *It's not about who won that argument or who lost out on that decision—it's about how well you both work together in a spirit of fairness and compromise.* Remember the Relationship Reality that stated that you can't get what you want all the time? The corollary to this reality is the idea that you can get *some* of what you want if you and your partner are willing to engage in a compromise.

The essence and beauty of a compromise is that, sure, you both give something up, but you also get something back in return. For instance, sometimes I get to watch sports on a Saturday afternoon, and my wife gets to have me take her out to dinner on Saturday night. Sometimes I don't feel like doing the household chores, but I do them anyway. In return, my wife will help pay the bills. I know that these are small examples, but every time we compromise, our relationship grows stronger. We get to work *with* each other, not *against* each other.

There are very few things that you simply *must have* in life. I'm not encouraging you to just give up if you really feel that a need must be met. If you define something as being vital to your happiness, then go for it, but don't act like a baby if things don't go your way. Whining and pouting are childish coping skills that don't help the relationship. Instead, work with your partner to find a way to get what you both want.

Think about compromise in a new way: You become a closer couple each time you and your partner reach a fair middle ground on an issue. *In a compromise, the relationship wins, which, after all, is the most important victory.*

Do you have the foundation of a great relationship? If you can answer the following five questions with a definitive yes, then you're well on your way.

1. Is your partner **consistent** in actions and words? Can you usually predict how your he or she will react in a variety of situations?

2. Is your partner **committed** to working through tough relationship problems and doing whatever it takes to make the relationship thrive?

3. Does your partner **care** about your feelings and value your beliefs?

4. Are you and your partner generally **compatible** in life interests and goals?

5. Are you and your partner willing to **compromise** once in a while and allow the other to take the lead?

You obviously don't need all of these qualities to have a fighting chance at a secure and stable relationship. But the more of these that are present, the better off you are. However, even if you score a perfect five out of five here, you still need to find a way to get along each day.

Now let's go one step further to perfect the art of another very important C: *communication.* How well do you cope with the inevitable problems that crop up in your relationship from time to time? Do you and your partner communicate in other ways besides talking? Can you defuse angry situations just by being on the same verbal frequency? Let's find out.

CHAPTER 18

Conquering Relationship Conflicts

LET'S NOW MOVE AHEAD WITH THE NEXT CRUCIAL STEP in creating a great relationship. *In this chapter, we'll develop a system that will help you strengthen your daily interactions with your partner.* You may have made a serious commitment and hope to spend the rest of your life with that "special someone," but first you have to get along on a daily basis!

We just finished discussing the Five C's of a healthy partnership—qualities that will increase your chance of success. This chapter could be titled "The Sixth C—Communication." I can't emphasize enough how important communication is in any relationship. For example, I know many fine people who loved each other and shared similar goals but couldn't stay together because they didn't have the communication skills to handle the inevitable frustrations and anger that arise in any relationship. When two people are together for any length of time, there are bound to be unmet expectations and hurt feelings—there's no way around this. *The key in determining a couple's success won't be found in how well they avoid conflicts, but in how well they handle them.*

I know that several books have been written describing the various differences between men and women as they interact in relationships. These books say that men have a certain set of emotions in common, and women have another. While there may be a certain amount of truth in this theory, my goal is to not focus on gender differences. I believe that there are certain *universal themes* that must be understood by *both* men *and* women. We have much more in common that we think when it comes to dealing with daily relationship obstacles. You can talk all day about the different ways of communicating, but that doesn't change the fact that you need to understand the mechanics—"the ABCs," if you will—of dealing with your partner.

Believe it or not, *emotions, behavior, and the thoughts behind both* are the components of *any* single interaction or conversation that you and your partner have together. Understanding each of these parts separately, as well as how they work together, is the key to maintaining a healthy, positive relationship.

I call these tools the *ABCs of any relationship experience.* We'll spend the first part of this chapter generally defining these ABCs; the second half will be devoted to applying them to situations in your relationship where anger or frustration are present. I chose anger and frustration specifically because these are the emotions that will tear a relationship wide open.

You must be able to understand your anger in a way that becomes manageable, or else there will be some real trouble ahead. Remember: *Difficulty in handling anger and conflicts is probably the greatest reason why relationships fail.* But I don't fault you, since you've most likely never been given specific techniques on how to resolve frustrating situations. By the end of this chapter, you'll have a firm understanding of what it takes to manage relationship challenges.

If your experience so far has been that relationships usually deteriorate into a mess of hurt feelings and anger, then you need a way to get some control—applying the ABCs can give you that control so that you and your partner never have to spend another day angry at each other without knowing how to make things better.

The ABCs of a Relationship Interaction

In the process of objectively analyzing your relationship experiences, you should use the following system so that the memory becomes more indelible—this applies to both men and women. In each case, each of these experiences has *three components* that you should attempt to recall and understand. For simplicity's sake, I refer to these components as "The ABCs of a Relationship Interaction," and you ought to apply them to problems in your relationship— whether you're having a minor argument or are on the verge of breaking up. This method is something I teach my patients, and it's quite useful. If you're able to figure out the ABCs of *any interaction* (past or present), you're well on your way to understanding yourself and your partner better, and your communication will improve greatly. Let's take a look at the ABCs in general and then apply the principles to the emotions of anger and frustration later on.

A: Affect

The *A* in *ABC* stands for *affect* (the noun), which is another term for your *emotions*. Sometimes the predominant thing that's manifested in a relationship experience is an emotion. For instance, have you ever been watching a TV show or movie that wasn't even very sad, yet you found yourself sobbing? What's happening is you're having an *emotional memory*. Something in your environment triggers a sensitive area deep inside you, and you spontaneously have an outpouring of feeling—which happens before you can even stop to think about it.

I'll bet that at some point you became very disappointed or angry with your partner and did or said something that you regretted later. You were so angry that the hurtful words just came out quickly, before you could censor your thoughts. And due to your emotional reaction, the relationship suffered. I've worked with many people who, in the heat of battle, have done incredibly stupid things. But when I ask them what thoughts accompanied their emotions, they often say, "I don't know."

A life experience that holds meaning over time will have an affect—or emotion—connected to it. Of course, I'm not referring to going to the grocery store—there aren't usually intense feelings attached to this or any other mundane, everyday routine. I'm talking about the occasions you feel *any* emotion—from sadness, frustration, anger, or jealousy, to euphoria, happiness, and joy. All of these things happen during any given relationship, and it's useful to recognize where they come from.

Keep in mind that *recognition is always the first step*—you must recognize that you're feeling something first, and only then can you seek to understand *why* you're having the emotion.

B: Behavior

Let's move on to the next component of relationship interactions: the *B,* which represents *behavior.* This is simply the outward physical manifestation of a thought or emotion—you act out what's going on inside your head by behaving a certain way. First, you have an emotion, which is followed by a characteristic behavior. Sometimes your partner will do things that make absolutely no sense, and it's easy to think that they're just plain crazy. Yet there's *always* a reason for any behavior, even those that seem completely out of left field or that threaten to ruin a relationship.

So we all have characteristic ways of behaving in response to a given situation. In any major event that has occurred in your current or past relationships, *there's always an affect, followed by a behavior.* I assume that most of your daily actions are not off the curve. For example, if your partner gets angry, you may fight back or withdraw. If you're suspicious of your partner, you may call to check up on him or her. This may *seem* like reasonable behavior, but acting this way can lead to difficulties in the relationship. So it's important to understand this behavior, even if on the surface it seems to be a completely sound response.

C: Cognition

The third component is the C, which represents *cognition*. This is just another way of expressing that there's a *thought* attached to any experience. You may feel anger toward your partner and your thought is to verbalize this, perhaps by saying, "I'm so upset with you!" On the other hand, from past experience, you may think that it's not right or helpful to say heated words to your partner because you think this will lead to more conflict. So your thought leads you to withdraw and not say what you really feel.

For most people, recognizing their actual thoughts is probably the easiest of the ABCs. Identifying emotions and analyzing your behavior is more difficult because it's something that most of us have never been challenged to do.

Using the ABCs in Everyday Life

Let's see if a common relationship problem can help us understand how the ABCs of communication work in everyday life.

Mandy and Eric are married. Eric wants to go out with some friends once a week—maybe to play some golf, go out to a restaurant, or attend a sporting event. But every time that he gets ready to leave, Mandy gets really upset. She asks him not to go, claiming that he's "leaving" her. Sometimes she cries; other times she becomes angry and jealous. Mandy accuses Eric of not wanting to be with her, and even goes so far as to imply that he's cheating on her. Eric simply can't understand why his going out is such a big deal, so he just ignores her or tells her to "back off"—he has absolutely no idea why she would overreact in this way, so his solution is to say, "What's the problem? I'm just going out with the guys. Stop being such a baby!"

"The problem is that you never pay any attention to me or care about how I feel!" Mandy retorts.

A huge argument ensues, exploding into a long fight about their relationship . . . all of this following a seemingly innocent desire by Eric to spend a little time with friends. (Of course, I make the assumption that there hasn't been a pattern of infidelity and deceit when Eric has previously gone out without Mandy. If there has, then her concerns would be reasonable and warranted.)

Let's apply the ABCs to this interaction and make sense out of *why* Mandy is so upset. The real reason why she has this negative response is because she has *a memory of a past experience that produces the ABCs of this interaction*, one that she may not be aware of. We'll deal with the past in a later chapter to find out where this memory came from, but first, let's understand the ABCs of Mandy's reaction.

A	B	C
Mandy's **emotion** of anger, fear, or jealousy that her husband is leaving her again	Mandy's **behavior** —trying to block the door, with-drawing, grab-bing her husband	Mandy's **thought** that she doesn't want Eric to leave

So that's it. As we look at Mandy and Eric's situation, it's certainly easier for us as outsiders to define the ABCs of this interaction than it is for Mandy. But for her relationship to go more smoothly—and in order to avoid this type of conflict in the future—Mandy (and Eric) first need to recognize and talk about the ABCs. Mandy would definitely benefit from using this system to understand why she became so irrational.

Remember, while Mandy is acting out her issues with Eric, he's also experiencing his own ABCs. Perhaps *his A* is anger that she's upset again, *B* is his behavior of leaving anyway and staying out late with his friends, and *C* is his thought that Mandy is insecure and a nag.

We've gone through the first step in understanding this negative interaction. Recognizing the emotions, behaviors, and thoughts attached to this particular situation will make it easier for Mandy and Eric to communicate and find a better way of coping. They could achieve success in their relationship and could change their way of arguing if they'd only stop to think about how they're behaving.

If Mandy were in my office, I'd take her through the following steps (which I've outlined thus far in this book):

1. Mandy needs to know that her **feelings of anger and jealousy have an origin,** and it's okay to *look within* for the answers. The reason why she feels so angry when Eric leaves is rooted in her life experiences in the *past* when she felt abandoned or slighted. Mandy's husband, friends, or family probably aren't going to be able to tell her why she's having this intense emotional reaction, but *she'll* be able to figure it out and subsequently make changes. Mandy absolutely

has the power to take control of her life. She can be her own relationship therapist if she's willing to objectively analyze her own reaction just as a third party (such as myself) would do. Her behavior isn't something to be embarrassed about; it's something to be understood.

2. Mandy needs to be **honest** in recounting her part of the exchange with Eric. Saying, "Oh, I wasn't that angry anyway," or "We'll get over it" isn't going to be helpful, and such comments minimize Mandy's distress and the consequences of her furious outbursts. Mandy needs to admit that there's a problem and that this problem could potentially ruin her relationship. She should acknowledge how she *really* feels—of course it would be tempting for her to omit details because, like all of us, she may feel ashamed of anger and insecurity—but true change will take place only after she sees things as they are and recognizes her behavior as something to be understood. Mandy and Eric's relationship will survive if they're able to openly talk about the problem and she honestly takes responsibility for her role in it—if Mandy communicates to Eric that her reaction is inappropriate to this moment, and that the problem may not be his. She needs to accept that even though her emotions may be displaced onto him, they're really about her past relationships and hurt feelings.

3. Mandy needs to use the ABCs in order to have a complete picture of the self-defeating cycle she and Eric have, for it would be virtually impossible for her to go on to the next steps if she wasn't able to recognize her emotions, thoughts, and resulting behavior. Mandy has to first attempt to faithfully recount her *exact* response to Eric leaving, so she can later understand how this **replays the same emotion from the past.** Maybe at some point in her life she experienced a similar situation—that is, someone left her and it hurt (I'll go into this phenomenon later on). Perhaps her father used to leave her mother alone frequently, or maybe a past boyfriend would cheat on Mandy when he left to go with "friends." For Mandy, the very act of leaving takes on the symbolic meaning that Eric doesn't love or value her.

Anger in the Relationship

As I promised earlier, we're now going to develop a process that you can use to deal with angry and frustrating situations. If you begin to use the ABCs in relationship conflicts, you can change the whole tone of your union from resentment to contentment. This one tool alone can actually make you and your partner much happier together—because anger will never get the best of you again. But first, let's briefly try to understand exactly why two people who love each other can get incredibly irate and frustrated, almost to the point of no return.

(Then, in the next section, we'll actually apply the ABCs.)

This is a given: *Unprocessed anger will ruin your life relationships.* Your relationship simply won't be any good if you and your partner can't deal with anger in a meaningful way. The way *not* to do it is to sweep the feelings away, hoping that things will just get better on their own. Sure, you both may forget about the argument a day later, but the feelings are still there, just waiting for another chance to attack.

The other way not to handle anger is to yell and scream at each other. If you give little thought or effort to understanding *why* things have gotten out of hand, you're in a world of hurt, because after harsh words are exchanged, most people don't tend to feel like going the extra mile to help their partner develop a better approach, or to make peace.

Let's briefly touch on where anger and hurt feelings in relationships stem from. Naturally, it's impossible for me to list every single reason why you or your partner might be upset, since each of you has different past experiences that set up the possibility of an angry outburst.

Many times in a relationship, anger is justified, but more often than not, it's an unreasonable response to a small thing. There's one common denominator in the origin of anger and frustration in a relationship, however: On some level, it's always based on the feeling of an *unmet expectation.*

The equation is simple: *We have an expectation that our partner doesn't meet, then we get angry and frustrated.* This is the origin of conflict in any relationship, and it doesn't matter how reasonable or insane our expectation is—if it's something that our minds tell us we need, we become upset when this need isn't met. In our mind, this process happens way before we get angry, behave in a certain way, or think certain thoughts about our partner. In other words, if the actual angry interaction with our partner (the ABCs) is like a car, then the unmet expectation is the fuel that drives that car in the first place.

Think about this for a minute: *What are your expectations of your partner? What are the things that are guaranteed to make you incensed if they're not present in your relationship?* It doesn't matter if these expectations are big or small. We all expect certain things that seem reasonable to us, and our partner will also expect things from us that *they* think are reasonable in return. The challenge comes when you two don't agree on the relative importance of these things to each other.

I don't know of any simple way to ensure that you'll never get upset with your partner for falling short of an expectation. Likewise, you'll also find yourself in the doghouse sometimes when *you* don't meet *their* needs. For example, you may think that it's a sensible expectation for your partner to help out with the dinner dishes each night—but your partner may not. Instead of becoming angry because you see your expectation as *reasonable,* while they see it as *unreasonable,* the solution lies in the old-fashioned way of *talking about what you want and what your partner wants.*

I realize that many arguments have no clear-cut answers, but here's an **exercise** that may help you immensely as you deal with frustration in your relationship. First, you and your partner should each make a chart called *Things I Expect to Happen or I Become Angry.* Be honest, and list everything that you can think of—the list may be rather long, but that's okay. The categories might include emotional/security needs, everyday household needs, romantic needs, financial needs, hygienic needs, communication needs, and so on.

Now, here's the tough part. For every single one of those things that you need from your partner, ask yourself the somewhat uncomfortable question: "Is this a *reasonable* request or an *unreasonable* request?" Your partner should do the exact same thing. Follow up this exercise by discussing what areas you agree and completely disagree on. Talking about these aspects of your relationship can be extremely rewarding.

Look, this isn't going to automatically solve all of your relationship problems, but at least it's a start. It forces both of you to consider whether your anger is justified, but it also forces you to take your partner's feelings and needs into account. This is the grunt work of a relationship, but it's well worth the effort. And if you both do this one exercise, I'll bet that the level of stress you feel in your union will decline, simply because you both can understand each other a little better. It will probably be harder to stay angry with your partner if you understand where they're coming from in the first place.

The ABCs of Anger

This section is extremely important, so please take your time with the following material. Your efforts here can pay off big time in your relationship because I'm

going to show you *a specific approach to managing anger.*
Unprocessed frustration between you and your partner will
not only destroy any chance of long-term happiness, but
it will make your time together unpleasant. It's time to
apply the ABCs to your relationship situations—which,
over the years, may have become filled with tension.

If you don't do anything else in this book, please do this
one **exercise!** And challenge your partner to do the same.

Start with five columns, and where I've drawn a blank,
fill in your own words. (You'll notice that the first three
columns are the aforementioned ABCs, and I've tacked on
two additional areas to focus on.)

A: Emotion	B: Behavior	C: Thoughts	D: Develop- ments	E: Effective Solutions
"I get angry/ frustrated when___ _____ _____" (regarding your partner).	"I do _____ _____ _____ when I feel upset about this."	"I then think _____ _____ about my partner or myself."	(Write down the results of what happens after A, B, and C.)	(Write down a better way of dealing with the problem.)

I suggest that you only write one set of five columns
(labeled A through E) per angry situation on each piece of
paper because you'll probably run out of room. If you only
did one of these exercises each day—that is, if you analyzed
one frustrating experience with your partner—you could
conceivably make great gains. So let's look at each column
in more detail.

1. Column A—Emotion

This constitutes the emotional, or affect column, so I want you to write down the situations in which you feel anger or frustration toward your partner. They can be minor things, such as "I get angry when he doesn't help with household chores"; or more serious things, such as "I get frustrated when he won't spend time with me or talk to me." The common denominator is the sentence, *"I get angry/frustrated when _____."*

I'm sure that you can easily think of dozens of things that your current (or past) partner does that provokes your emotions. Let your imagination go—anytime you're consciously aware of anger or frustration can count. The issues can include anything from finances, communication, your sex life, differences in parenting styles, bad habits, family problems, or just the fact that your partner doesn't work at the relationship as much as you do. If you can't recognize your emotions, ask your partner or someone close to you to help fill out this list—I'm sure that they'll be more than happy to give you their input!

2. Column B—Behavior

Next, describe *your* behavior—which results from each of the situations in the first column. For instance, perhaps you wrote down in Column A that *"I get angry when my husband criticizes my appearance,"* so in Column B, ask the question, *"What do I do when I feel upset about this?"* Describe your exact behavior in response to your angry feelings. In this case, would you yell at your husband? Would you withdraw and think that you were wearing the wrong

clothes? Would you refuse to go out? Would you silently
stew and not speak to your husband the rest of the night?
Would you act out, perhaps by becoming intoxicated?
You may have a variety of responses, but try to figure out
the most common behavior you're likely to exhibit. It's crucial that you *honestly acknowledge the exact behavior,*
no matter how offensive or embarrassing you think it is.

Also be aware that the behavior you remember may
not necessarily be accurate. For example, I know that my
wife gets angry with me for being late. When we did this
exercise, she acknowledged in Column A that my tardiness
makes her feel frustrated. However, in Column B, she
put down "nothing" as her behavior. She isn't aware of
doing anything in particular when she's perturbed with me
about my lateness—yet I know from experience that this
is simply not the case. She certainly has a characteristic way
of behaving toward me when I'm chronically late! When
we talked about this, she was able to learn from me how
she reacts. I was able to help her, and in the process, we
also communicated about an issue that impacts both of us
in our relationship. The lesson here is that you may not be
able to judge your own behaviors, so ask your partner how
you really do act when you're upset.

3. Column C—Thoughts

In this column, put down any thoughts that you
experience after you become upset or angry: *"I think
_____ about my partner"* or *"I think
_____ about myself."* Continuing with the
previous example, if you get angry toward your husband for
criticizing your appearance, and you've identified that you

withdraw and don't confront him—what do you then think about yourself? Do you think that you're ugly? Do you think that no one will ever be attracted to you again? Do you think that your husband is a jerk? Or do you think that you'll wear whatever you want and still feel good about yourself?

Your thoughts are extremely important because they ultimately define who you are and how you'll interact with your world. People who chronically think poorly about themselves have a very difficult time keeping relationships together, since their low self-esteem and pessimistic thinking frequently get in the way. Many authors have noted that *negative thoughts create negative outcomes in relationships:* Your thoughts are a self-fulfilling prophecy, so thinking over and over that you'll be abandoned and the relationship will end ironically makes it more likely that this will occur.

The other thing to note in this column is the aftermath of your thoughts: What do you actually *say* to your partner when you're upset? Many relationships have ended simply because one person can't keep quiet and feels compelled to say hurtful things to their partner. It's not always wise to express whatever comes to mind in a moment of anger. Some of the most successful people in relationships have the skill of knowing what *not* to say. Have you ever said really nasty things to your partner because your feelings got hurt? And then did you regret what you said because most of it wasn't true?

Each of us knows the one thing that our partner feels ashamed or embarrassed about, and that could easily be the most powerful piece of ammunition in a fight. Focusing on this thing may effectively end the argument— but it may ultimately ruin the relationship, as well. Phrases such as "I hate you!" or "You're such a loser—you can't do anything right!" or "I'm leaving you right now!" can have a lasting effect on the relationship. There are lots of other variations of these statements, but it all boils down to one theme: You're angry, you think hurtful thoughts, and you direct these damaging words toward your partner. Or perhaps your partner does this to you. Maybe you both make up later, but every time you say malicious things to one another, the relationship is that much closer to ending.

Try to think before you speak! Emotionally charged statements are rarely going to enhance your relationship, so take some time to cool down—before you say something that can never be taken back. Also remember that *the angry words you shout are usually not about your partner, but someone else has used those words against you at some point in your past.*

The most effective thing to say when you're angry is simply, "You made me feel _____, and I'd like us to figure out why we just had this interaction." You don't have to use those exact words, but this statement allows you to verbalize your feelings and open the door for productive communication. If your partner doesn't initially respond to this, then it's okay to back off and try again later when the situation is calmer.

4. Column D—Developments

The next logical event in our sequence is represented by Column D. The *D* stands for *developments*. If you get upset, behave in a certain way, and think certain things, then there will naturally be an end result. What actually develops from an altercation with your partner? Do you both begin to yell and scream at each other, while nothing of substance gets accomplished? Do you always give in and take the blame or say that you're sorry, even when it's not your fault? Do you or your partner engage in the old "silent treatment" and not speak to each other for hours . . . or even days? Or do you, like a lot of couples, just sweep your issues under the rug and hope that the tension goes away, without ever really processing the hurt feelings?

For each interaction you've identified above, there will usually be a characteristic way that you and your partner handle the conflict. Unfortunately, the development is usually based on each partner's immediate need to avoid any further anxiety, or to get in the last word and feel as if their stance was "right." When enough of these angry interactions add up over time, without a positive resolution, the relationship suffers. It becomes defined as two people who just can't get along, who are always frustrated and angry at each other, and who live day-to-day through a series of unresolved arguments. Then the saying "There's too much water under the bridge" comes into play—there comes a point of no return, because the couple never sat down and critically analyzed these events, nor did they ever try to develop ways of making things better.

So it's necessary for you and your partner to honestly identify what actually happens in your relationship when there's anger or hurt feelings. That's what this column is about: *writing down what happens when you're upset*, so that we can then move ahead to the next column, which deals with techniques to make things work better.

5. Column E—Effective Solutions

This column challenges you to consider other coping techniques that could be more effective than the ones you typically use. The *E* stands for creating an *effective* solution to an angry conflict. Up to this point, you've identified something that makes you angry (Column A), how you behave in response to your anger (Column B), what you think about your partner (Column C), and what then actually develops as a result (Column D).

The next most likely step is that you and your partner will revert back to your old, unproductive ways of dealing with anger and frustration, and your attempts to actually solve the problem will make things even more frustrating. It's a vicious circle that goes around and around, with the outcome becoming the new problem! You may not even remember what the initial argument was about, as the new conflict will now center on how you both argue. But it doesn't have to be that way! So, before we get to how we can change our old ways of resolving conflicts, let's first take a look at what *not* to do.

An Example of the ABCs in Action

Here's a simple example that illustrates how, when both partners utilize ineffective coping skills, things can go rapidly downhill.

Matt opens up the monthly credit card statement and sees that his wife, Kim, has again spent a lot of their money without telling him first. He spends all evening stewing before she returns home from a friend's house.

Watch how their discussion unfolds and ends up far from the original complaint:

1. Column A: The Emotional/*Affect*ive Exchange

Matt (angrily): "You did it again! You ran up our credit cards, and you know we don't have the money."

Kim: "Yes, we do. You just got paid!"

Matt: "That's not the point. You didn't tell me you were going to buy these things."

Kim: "So I have to ask permission before I can do anything?"

2. Column B: The Conversation Shifts to Behavioral Mode; Both People Act Out

Matt: "Yes! You need to call me before you use any credit cards again!"

Kim: "I'm not going to call you. You're not my mother!"

Matt (grabbing a pair of scissors): "Well, then just give me the card. I'm going to cut it up!"

Kim (runs into the other room): "No, you won't! I'll hide it from you."

3. Column C: Cognitive—They Verbalize Hurtful Thoughts Without Thinking

Matt: "I can't believe you're so greedy! You don't need all those clothes."

Kim: "Well, if you *really* cared about me, you'd buy me something once in a while. I always have to buy things for myself!"

Matt: "Like you do anything for me! We haven't had sex in over a month. I'm sick and tired of everything being about you!"

Kim (slamming the door): "You are such a jerk!"

4. Column D: What Develops As a Result of Ineffective Communication?

Matt and Kim spend the rest of the evening in separate rooms, not talking to each other. They get up the next morning, and Matt leaves for work, while Kim feels guilty and returns all of the clothes she bought. When Matt comes home that evening, the subject is dropped—neither is willing to broach the credit card issue, fearing another angry confrontation.

5. Column E: What Would Have Been a More Effective Way of Interacting?

I'm sure that you can look back at this disastrous interaction and identify many mistakes made by both Matt and Kim, but in the heat of battle, it's much more difficult to take a step back and observe one's own behavior. It's so difficult, in fact, that there's little chance of righting yourself midstream unless you've consciously thought about more effective coping skills *beforehand*. So let's state the number-one rule for an effective interaction: *You must think about how to handle a conflict in your relationship before it happens, for if you allow your emotions to get the best of you, it's all over.*

It's easy to see in the above confrontation that both Kim and Matt get emotional and say and do things that they probably don't mean to do. Matt calls Kim "greedy"; she calls him a "jerk." They start out with a problem about managing their money and finish by yelling about other disappointments (lack of attention and sex). Matt initially approaches Kim in the wrong way because he starts angrily accusing her right off the bat, but Kim follows this up by failing to address his concern, as she gets defensive and goes into the counterattack mode. The initial problem gets lost in the shuffle after they both react instinctively and emotionally to the other. The original issue—the very important one of money management—is never even discussed in any reasonable way. Other potential problems, such as Matt and Kim's intimacy, are subsequently thrown into the mix, only adding fuel to the fire.

How could Matt and Kim have handled this interaction in order to achieve a better outcome? After all, once they got started, there was probably nothing that could have averted the train wreck. So the key for them would have been to do some *preventative* work, *prior to the argument.* They should have considered some alternative ways to deal with the disagreements that naturally arise in any relationship, but they didn't do their homework and the result was regrettable.

More Effective Ways to Deal with Anger

I'm now going to help you create some basic ways to effectively manage conflicts in your relationship. As I said, it's simply not possible to account for every single type of emotional response or disagreement, but there are some general principles that can make your life a whole lot easier with your partner. Going back to your "E column," carefully consider these things—you'll save yourself a lot of relationship woes.

First of all, make a pact with your partner that you both strictly promise not to break for any reason: *Agree that neither of you will use derogatory names toward each other during an argument or heated situation.* A lot of couples end up hating each other simply because they've said so many nasty and hurtful things to each other over the years. Name-calling takes its toll on a relationship by making a lack of mutual respect an accepted part of your interactions. If you do accidentally let an insult slip out, immediately apologize to your partner on the spot. Challenge yourself to say, "I'm sorry for that. I didn't mean to call you a _____." You can do this! It's not impossible.

Next, vow to each other that you'll attempt to stay centered on the original complaint and *deal with one complaint at a time.* If you veer off into other sensitive areas, nothing will ever get resolved. The reason why so many couples feel unsatisfied at the end of a discussion is because they try to deal with too many frustrations at once and don't focus on just one topic. For instance, if you're upset about a money issue, try to stay on that one particular topic. I know it's difficult to do, but it's not impossible! If you or your partner start to derail the conversation, catch yourself by saying, "Let's deal with _____ now and get to _____ later."

Finally, *know when to say when*. You'll have accomplished little by beating a dead horse. The longer an argument lasts, the greater the chance that it will degenerate into an exasperated shouting match. It's just a part of life that sometimes you can't get your way, no matter how emotional you become. If your partner says that they want to stop talking for a while, back off and approach them later. Sometimes you can't make your partner believe what you believe, so, instead of always trying to change them, why not work toward a compromise? *It's okay to agree to disagree.* You and your partner can still have a loving, respectful union without always agreeing on everything.

Even if you follow these "rules of engagement," you may still have difficulty resolving your anger and frustration. I urge you to share these principles with your partner, but if they become a raving lunatic during a disagreement, there may not be much you can do to solve your problems. If they continue to be irrational and disrespectful, ask them to consider that this may be a manifestation of some past issue in their life. If they won't even allow for this possibility, then you should be prepared for a roller coaster of a relationship, which may not end well.

A Summary of the ABCs

Let's quickly recap the ABCs of interacting. I know that this can get confusing, and it isn't my intent to complicate your life even further, or to provide you with an unwieldy system that you'll never use. If you give it a chance, you'll find that the ABCs really aren't that difficult to apply to everyday life situations. There's no other effective way I know of for you to understand and correct the things that tend to end relationships— out-of-control affects, behaviors, and thoughts directed at your partner or yourself.

Whenever a disagreement arises in your relationship that could lead to a heated exchange, you should automatically remember to do the ABCs. This can be accomplished in a matter of seconds, but will force you into the practice of analyzing your own psychology.

- First, what are you feeling? **What is your predominant affect (the A)?** Are you happy, sad, angry, disappointed? There are literally hundreds of emotions that you could experience in the course of a relationship, so start to acknowledge your own range of feelings.

- Second, **how are you behaving in response to the emotion (the B)?** What do you do when you feel something strongly? Put a lot of your energy here into analyzing what you *do* when you're upset with your partner.

- Third, **what thoughts go through your head (the C)**, either about yourself or your partner? Do you only think negative thoughts about your relationship, or are you able to see a glimmer of light even in the throes of anger? Again, it will be especially helpful to categorize your thoughts when you're upset or angry.

- Fourth, when there's a conflict in the relationship, **what develops between you and your partner (the D)?** Do you see a predominant pattern of a certain response to a certain emotion? For instance, is there one thing that seems to keep happening when you and your partner are upset?

- Fifth, **is there a more effective way for you both to handle relationship conflicts (the E)?** It may actually be fun to sit down with your partner and ask the question, *"What can we do differently to get along better with each other?"* It's not a bad idea to talk with your partner about how you could express emotions in a way that preserves respect for you both. A loss of respect between partners is one of the major reasons why a relationship falls apart, but it doesn't suddenly appear— it has to start somewhere and usually begins in subtle ways during arguments.

Please start to think about your life relationships in this new way. The very next time that you have the urge to say something hurtful to your partner, stop yourself and remember that you once felt tremendous love and warmth for them. Ask yourself, *"Do I really want to spend my life focusing on negativity in my relationships?"*

When I did this for myself, there was a marked change in the quality of my interactions. Sure, I still have strong emotions that I need to process with my wife, but the *tone* has changed. After all, when the dust clears from a moment of difficulty, what's really left behind? You and your partner still have to find effective ways of dealing with each other.

I could have called Column E *empathy* because putting yourself in your partner's shoes and imagining how they feel is absolutely the most effective way to handle a relationship conflict. I know that I claimed that there were no "secrets" to making a relationship work, but empathy is absolutely crucial in a relationship. After all, at the end of the day, if you and your partner can't understand where the other person is coming from, or have no clue how they feel, then you really don't have much of a chance to create a happy and secure union.

Remember that relationships can only exist as a result of two people making a commitment to be *kind* to each other. In the final analysis, it doesn't matter that you and your partner may want different things, or that your partner drives you crazy now and again, or that you can't remember the ABCs of your interactions every time. All that really matters is a covenant between partners, based on *kindness*. If you ask yourself the following question several times a day, you'll improve your union (as well as just being a nicer person): *"What can I do this very second to practice kindness to myself and the person whom I love?"* You won't believe the difference it can make in your relationship.

CHAPTER 19

What's Love
Got to Do with It?

*L*OVE. IT'S AMAZING THAT THIS ONE LITTLE WORD CAN
account for so much joy *and* heartbreak in the world.
Love truly is the cement that bonds two people together,
and relationships can't flourish without it. After all, the
reason that you join another person in a serious, monog-
amous union in the first place is because you love them and
would be miserable without them in your life. And since
I'm writing a book about relationships, I'd be remiss if I
didn't include some thoughts about love.

In the last chapter, we developed some ways to understand anger. We looked at some useful coping skills and
classified affects, behaviors, and thoughts. But unfortunately, it's impossible to "cope" with love—for most people,
it's something that just "is."

So you may be puzzled as to why we need to tackle the nearly insurmountable task of analyzing the love in your relationship—after all, haven't thousands of songs, poems, quotes, and movies quite adequately described it? But since love hits us individually at our deepest levels of hope and fear, it's a subject that will never go away and will always remain something of a mystery.

The questions are numerous: *Will I ever fall in love? What happened to the love that my partner and I once had? What if I love someone and they don't love me back? Now that my relationship has ended, will I ever find love again? How can my mate and I stay in love forever?* These are the essential issues that every single one of us will face in the course of creating a lifetime partnership with another human being. Without an intensely strong emotional tie to your partner, you'll be hard-pressed to keep things alive in the relationship. But just what *is* that feeling? Is it really love that keeps you coming back for more, or is it something else?

I was talking to my friend Cheryl, when, out of the blue, she proudly announced that she'd "fallen in love." I was a bit wary, since she'd only known Juan for a few weeks. She was excitedly describing their wonderful dates and talking of marriage when I injected the voice of reality.

I simply asked, "How do you know you're in love?"

She replied, with some indignation, "Well, I just do! Juan said that he loved me, and I said that I loved him, too."

I pressed on. "But what exactly *is* love to you?"

"It's . . . it's just incredible," stammered Cheryl. "I've never felt like this about anyone before."

Cheryl never really did answer my question, but she then turned around and accused me of trying to ruin everything by once again overanalyzing her feelings in a psychiatric way (which, I'll concede, may or may not be true).

As Cheryl walked away, I reminded her to just be cautious, because she'd hastily "loved" other men in the past and things had ended just as quickly as they'd begun. She said that she would take this into consideration, but I knew that her heart was saying otherwise. . . . Cheryl had been bitten by the love bug.

A bite from this particular creature characteristically releases a flood of symptoms that most of us can recognize: A pounding heart, pain in the pit of the stomach, sweaty palms, an impulse to do things completely out of character—all these things must mean you're utterly head-over-heels in love. Or are you? This is the critical question that we'll look at in this chapter.

What Is Love?

It's amazing that millions of us stake our chance at happiness on an emotion that's so difficult to define . . . and maybe we shouldn't even attempt to. I know that *I* can't adequately pinpoint the true essence of such a powerful feeling between two people.

When two people say that they love one another, what are they really saying? I went to the dictionary and looked up the word *love*. The official definition is a "strong attachment," and there were secondary meanings, such as "an intense liking of someone else." It became evident to me that it's enormously challenging to define *love* without using the word *love!*

I suppose that most folks would be satisfied to just say they've been "in love," and it made their relationship a wonderful experience—so why even bother with a rather academic exercise regarding this concept? After all, there's no argument regarding the fact that love is the crucial emotion in determining whether a relationship will survive or not, and there's no denying that loving someone else is a basic human experience that ties all of us together. But the key distinction is this: *Love is obviously a strong tie to your partner, but this attachment may be grounded in other outside factors.* In other words, you may be having an intense feeling that you *think* is love, but it's actually something else very different. *There are many reasons why you would choose to stay with a certain partner, many of which have nothing to do with "love."*

Do you remember the Tina Turner song "What's Love Got to Do with It"? I believe that love certainly *does* have a lot to do with it, but I'll also take the unromantic position that love is *not* the only intangible that keeps you attached to your partner.

I became absolutely convinced of this theory by hearing hundreds of sad and disturbing relationship stories over the years. The themes are always the same: Partner A "loves" Partner B, even through B is abusive, cheats, lies, or isn't invested in the relationship. Partner A will sometimes admit to the relationship flaws, but continues to hang on to B in the name of "love." Partner A has fallen for B and has the notion that if you "love" someone, you must put up with destructive behaviors that would end other relationships. Furthermore, A may also believe that if he/she just "loves" B enough, B will see the light and change for the better. You know how the story ends—A is really unhappy but claims "love" as an excuse to stay put.

So why is Partner A *really* attracted to someone who isn't good relationship material? First, let me make this clear:

Partner A certainly may have legitimate fondness for, and may appreciate certain characteristics about, B. After all, if there were no positives in their relationship, it would most likely end quickly. But we can see that A's "love" for B isn't the whole story. There must be *other dynamics* at work here that draw these two people together like magnets—even though the relationship itself isn't functioning well.

Before we get further into what love *isn't*, let's take a look at how someone behaves when they truly do love you. (Of course, this is *my* vision of love—others may see things differently—but I believe that this represents a mainstream concept.) What I mean is that if you or your partner don't exhibit the following qualities, there probably isn't enough love present to make this relationship last for a lifetime.

These qualities are present in someone who *really loves* you:

1. **Your partner cherishes and values you above all other people and things.** You're loved unconditionally on a day-to-day basis—and you feel this love constantly, no matter what obstacles and relationship difficulties you may be facing. You feel accepted for who you are, and don't feel that you have to change in order to conform to your partner's likes or dislikes.

2. **You're number one.** This simply means that your partner constantly strives to make your personal happiness a top priority. You're treated with respect and dignity every single

day. Your partner will value you and listen to what you have to say, even if there's a disagreement.

3. **You and your partner live by the code, "*What would be the* kind *thing to do right now*?"** Love is a complex emotion, but I do know that it must involve kindness and respect. Believe me, there will be many times during the course of your relationship that you and your mate will come up with entirely different solutions to a problem. Sometimes you'll get your way, and sometimes you won't—that's just part of dealing with another person. Someone who really loves you unconditionally, though, will always do the most *kind* and *respectful* thing on your behalf. If this situation is not currently the case, then you should think twice about your relationship.

4. **Someone who really loves you *never* intentionally hurts you.** This seems obvious, but some people have a difficult time understanding this concept. This means your partner doesn't cheat or do things behind your back that could destroy the relationship; doesn't make you look foolish in front of others; and doesn't say mean and nasty things that are designed to make you feel bad about yourself. I'm sure I've forgotten other ways that you could get your feelings hurt, but the point is that if your partner knows your sensitivities, he or she practices

kindness. In other words, your partner continually strives to make you feel good about yourself.

5. **Finally, if someone really loves you, their behavior matches their words.** It's one thing to say "I love you," but it's much more important to live this each day in your actions. Words count, but *behavior* will ultimately determine how much your partner really loves you. If your partner often treats you in an abusive and disrespectful way, but periodically says the magic words "I love you," is this truly a loving relationship? No, it's not. It's quite easy to fall into this relationship trap because we all want to believe our partner's words. But remember that words ring hollow unless they're followed up by the appropriate action. Don't be fooled into accepting some flowers or a fancy dinner as compensation for a pattern of relationship neglect by your mate. Also, if your partner does something terrible that could ruin the relationship but says "I'll never do it again," then they better never do it again. If they do, I don't know how their behavior could possibly be construed as love.

Be brutally honest with yourself here: Have you ever received love in the five ways listed above? Is this what you're getting from your partner? If so, you've probably struck relationship gold. If you're not receiving these things but you continue to stay with your partner, there may be *other reasons* to explain why you're with that person that have very little to do with love.

Love vs. Lust

Think about this dilemma for a moment: What would you do if you were with someone who made you unhappy in most areas of the relationship but was great in bed? Your decision would be to either move on to someone else, or to stay with a person whom you lusted after physically. Could you give up dynamite sexual chemistry because everything else in the relationship was mediocre? This is an interesting question that has yielded surprising results in several surveys. There's a percentage of the population that feels that a relationship based on physical attraction can survive, and I tend to believe these findings. The physical infatuation can be so intense that two people are unable to break free from each other, and when asked why they don't move on, their response is usually along the lines of, "I don't think I'll ever find anyone else I'm this attracted to."

Each of us has surface preferences (certain qualities we find physically or sexually attractive) that, when found in another person, are irresistible. You could argue that it's a product of biology, cultural bias, or media influence. But regardless of the cause, physical factors determine whether we'll even talk to someone in the first place, much less date them. The end result is that *lust is often confused with love, leading to relationships with significant difficulties.*

I'm reminded of a phone call that once came in to my

radio show. A woman explained that she immediately "fell in love" with a man when their eyes met across the room, and although she was now suffering through a devastating relationship with this man, she just couldn't get beyond the memory of that intense first moment, which had made such a powerful impression on her that she essentially ignored months of subsequent unhappiness. She spent her days desperately searching for another magical moment, even though none was to be had.

We argued for several minutes because she maintained her belief that what she'd experienced was true, lasting love. She'd become blind to the reality of her relationship, but she continued to hang on. This poor woman simply couldn't accept that she'd made the huge mistake of confusing a *lustful* moment with a *loving* moment—nor could she grasp that lust alone can't sustain a relationship over the long haul.

I firmly believe that *love can only develop over time.* I've debated this point with many colleagues who hold that "love at first sight" is possible. I've countered with the argument that, if this is the case, it *cheapens* the meaning of love. I feel this way because to me, love is a *process* that happens between two people, not a singular moment in time.

Love involves a commitment. Love is a feeling that the other person matters as much as or more than anything else in the world to you. Now think about this: After you've met someone for the first time or went out on a few dates, could you truthfully say to yourself that you would give up anything for that person? I find it highly unlikely that this is the case.

You may be in *"lust* at first sight," playing out a dynamic that won't hold the relationship together without other more important factors being present as well. The danger here is that walking around with stars in your eyes may blind you to the things you *need* in a healthy, loving, lifelong relationship.

On the other hand, lust is certainly necessary for a union to function well. Without any sexual sparks, your relationship could deteriorate into a mere friendship, as opposed to a romantic connection. The critical distinction, however, is that two people who base their relationship on a mostly physical attraction may ignore the work needed to promote a "love" connection. Staying with someone just because you think that they're "hot" is an error that could lead to a shallow and unfulfilling love life.

Transferring Old Emotions to Your Current Partner

I understand that in the course of reading a book there are many parts that you soon forget—*but this section should not be one of those parts.* If you remember nothing else about *A Relationship for a Lifetime,* then make it a point to read and reread this section in detail! What we're going to focus on next *forms the basis for your decisions about a life partner.* As promised in the Introduction, we'll now attempt to understand the reasons *why* you've chosen certain partners and may have stayed in an unfulfilling relationship.

There are forces other than love that cause you to be pulled toward another person in an almost magnetic way—this isn't just my theory, it's a fact grounded in basic psychology. For the most part, these forces operate on an unconscious level, so you're probably not even aware of their significance. And sometimes they even propel you into making great relationship choices.

However, if you have trouble breaking away from a

destructive or unhappy relationship, then love probably isn't what's keeping you together. If you keep repeating the same painful scenarios with different partners, then you've got some psychological issues from the past that must be analyzed and understood. *An intense, powerful attraction to another person is often just a replay of experiences from your past, and has little to do with love.* Unless you come to terms with these old, unresolved issues, you'll probably continue to make the same relationship mistakes over and over again.

To state it bluntly: *Your past counts!* It counts so much, in fact, that the field of psychology has devoted a condition to it called *transference.* My colleagues and I often discuss transference, but I doubt that you've ever even heard the word before. It's actually a fairly complicated topic, but it can be explained like this: *Transference is the process of projecting old feelings and behaviors on a current partner instead of on the person to whom these feelings were originally directed.* Believe me, this type of behavior in a relationship is responsible for a lot of breakups! A transference attraction to someone else may sometimes include love, but most times it's centered on the old baggage that we all bring into adulthood.

To really understand this concept, you first need to accept that you've carried some unresolved issues around with you for a very long time. Even if you feel pretty good about yourself and have been successful at relationships, it's worthwhile to take a look at some of your old patterns of behavior. I hope that I thoroughly made the point in previous chapters that you can only feel and act on the basis of what you knew from the past. Transference is merely your attempt to create what's *familiar* to you, both in positive and negative ways.

Therefore, *transference* will set the stage for the following in relationships:

1. *You will choose a partner based on previous relationship experiences.* Most likely, you'll end up recreating some aspect of your experiences from childhood with your parents or primary caretakers. You could also recreate a previous love experience from adulthood if this was painful enough to make a lasting impression on you.

2. After you've chosen a partner, *transference will also cause you to feel and behave in characteristic ways,* just as if the new partner is symbolically taking the place of the original person (parent, caretaker, or previous love interest).

I can't emphasize how important it is for you to understand these concepts! No one is immune from transference, because our minds naturally seek out what's familiar and try to attain it. For instance, the person who stays with an abusive partner has commonly experienced an abusive child-parent relationship or seen parents or caregivers mistreat each other. This is transference—choosing a new partner in adult life that recreates the old experience. In this way, a person can continue to act out the same old feelings and behavior, because it's what they know.

We'll get into more specific situations in the next chapter, but suffice it to say that *we'll always act in a way that makes sense to us, even if that path leads to sadness and pain.* One constant is that human beings always try to set up relationships in a way that is familiar and makes the most sense. Translating this to a practical level, I can safely state the following natural law of any relationship: *If you've seen or experienced mostly negative things in your previous relationships, you'll probably keep setting things up to mirror these experiences.*

I'm sure you're thinking that this seems like a completely crazy idea, since it seems logical that one would want to veer away from creating more unpleasant experiences. Why would someone want to keep doing things in a new relationship that never worked in past ones? It almost seems like a masochistic way to go through life. The reason is simple: The tendency for our brains to seek out an old, familiar situation is much greater than the tendency to seek out a new experience, which would be unfamiliar. *Changing a way of thinking about yourself and others is much more difficult than just staying the same.* Even if interacting in a new way in your relationship would be better, there's a good chance that you'll still follow the old pattern. This really just restates the physics law concerning *inertia* (an object going on a certain course will naturally tend to stay on that course, unless something else intervenes). In your case, the process of becoming aware of your past can serve as that intervention, propelling you on to a better and more satisfying relationship course.

By looking at a brief example, we can see how this process unfolds early in a relationship. Let's take a look at my friend Cheryl (from above) again. Her pattern is to seek out men who are hot and heavy at the beginning of a relationship but then pull away and eventually dump her without apparent reason. Although Cheryl knows on some level that her relationships are unsatisfying, she continues to be magnetically attracted to men who initially over-whelm her with their ardor. Now, it would be reasonable to assume that at some point, her brain would learn that a man who rapidly and intensely lavishes her with attention may be a partner who will just as quickly leave her, and hopefully she'd ascertain that those types of relationships should be avoided because they only lead to heartbreak.

But instead of learning this lesson, Cheryl's brain continues to seek out guys who will make her feel like the center of the universe at the onset of the relationship, even though it will lead to pain later on. It's as if she can't stop herself from continuing down this same old, familiar road.

Cheryl should ask herself these questions: "Why is it such a powerful experience to have someone else quickly smother me with attention?" and "Why is this familiar to me (what does this represent out of my past)?"

Cheryl's answers to these questions would lead her to understand that she's *transferring* a *past* issue onto a *present* one. I'll bet that she felt smothered by important people from her past, or she saw people in her life enacting this same dynamic with each other. Or perhaps she spent many years fantasizing what it would be like to feel wanted because she never got any affection growing up. Either way, Cheryl's brain sees hasty and overwhelming affection as a familiar pattern, and does whatever it has to do to get it.

The *transference (familiar experience)* can thus come about for two opposing reasons:

1. What Cheryl is going through in her adult relationships is *actually what she saw and/or experienced* in her past important life relationships (it's familiar to her).

2. She didn't get much affection or attention in
    the past, but she constantly *fantasized* about
    it, until it became a familiar pattern.

Hopefully, Cheryl will end up acknowledging her
tendency to fall prey to a flood of affection in the beginning of a relationship, and this will lead her to try to figure out why she keeps repeating old patterns from the past.
Then she'll be able to act objectively when it comes to
choosing a partner because she'll be basing her decision on
intellect, rather than past unresolved emotions.

A Visual Image of Your Past

I think you'll have no problem understanding the concept of transference if you just keep the following visual
image in mind.

Imagine yourself standing in front of your partner
with your eyes closed. Nothing has happened yet between
the two of you, and there's no one else there—it's just the
two of you in an empty room. Then your partner does or
says something (for example, they blame you for a relationship difficulty), a verbal or physical exchange follows,
and you feel terrible.

Imagine that the energy you and your partner have
created from this altercation is a giant sphere that is heading right for you. It hits you with a jolt, and the force radi-
ates throughout your body—yet this energy seems to have
stirred up something deep down inside of you that's been
festering, representing a sensitivity from the past that
you've never resolved. This "hot spot" you have within you
causes an immediate reaction based on emotions, not

logic. Although you sincerely want to handle the unpleas-
antness between you and your partner in a healthy way,
something is stopping you.

You open your eyes and are astonished to not only find
your partner in the room, but the ghosts of your parents,
family members, and ex-partners as well. They're all standing around you in a semicircle, and their energy is identical
to your partner's. *Everyone* starts throwing big energy balls
at you from all directions—and you can't stop it.
Consequently, you feel bad about yourself and begin to
retaliate.

But guess what? These people from your past are only
visible to *you*. Your partner can't see them—they can
only see your reaction as something directed straight
toward them or your relationship. So, instead of throwing
the energy back to the people in the past (where it belongs),
you've transferred it to your present relationship with
your partner. *You've transferred an old coping skill that
didn't work into a new coping skill that still doesn't work.*

You turn around . . . and poof! Your parents, ex-
lovers, and family members have all disappeared in a
cloud of smoke. You and your partner are once again
alone in the room. But now things have changed—thanks
to *your* past, you *both* have just had a terrible experience.
Your past got in the way of an interaction that could
have changed that negative energy into positive energy.

Then the lightbulb goes on over your head and you
realize that perhaps there were factors other than "love"
that caused you to choose this particular person to have
a relationship with. *Maybe you need to understand how
those ghosts from your past pushed you in a certain
direction with your partner.* Choosing this partner in the
first place was probably an attempt to go back to an old,

familiar childhood experience, and once you realize this, you can do the necessary work to stop repeating the same pattern indefinitely.

In the next chapter, we'll try to make sense of the adverse experiences you may have had while growing up. You're never going to escape the past, but you sure can change the negative energy that surrounds it so it doesn't affect your current relationship.

Don't let the ghosts get the last laugh.

CHAPTER 20

Ghosts from the Past

CONTINUING ON WITH LAST CHAPTER'S THEME, IT'S important that we come to the conclusion that the relationships we're creating right now are merely a culmination of life patterns established long ago.

I can't imagine that anyone would argue with me on this point, yet most of us who suffer through unfulfilling relationships often act as if the past doesn't matter at all. We say things such as, "Well, that's over and I'm done thinking about it!" or "I'm putting that relationship behind me." Old relationships are ostensibly forgotten as we move on to new things—as if the past is something to be "put away" and not acknowledged for its impact on current experiences.

The mistake here is that if we don't take the time to systematically analyze what went wrong in our past relationships, we're going to continue to be unfulfilled. Those of us with unsatisfying relationships make the critical error of viewing life as a series of disconnected events, rather than *seeing the past as something that sets the stage for all of our future relationships*. So, we proceed to go out and repeat the very same mistakes, and we're left wondering why things didn't turn out differently *this* time around.

Of course, no one would ever say that processing the pain from an unpleasant situation in the past is fun, but it's necessary. Since our beliefs drive our patterns of interaction and determine success or failure in our relationships, it's imperative to figure out where they stem from. So in this chapter, we'll do just that.

Moving Past Your Past

You may not yet be convinced that an objective analysis of your baggage is needed in order to increase your odds of present success; I even know of some professional therapists who disagree with me about this. They want their patients to live in the "here-and-now," and feel as if nothing is to be gained by digging around in someone's past. There's certainly nothing inherently harmful with their approach, but I feel that it short-changes the patient.

I often use the following analogy to explain my views on this subject. If you were driving down the road and had a flat tire, you'd have three options:

1. **You could keep driving, ruin your rim, and eventually be completely stuck.** Sheer common sense would cause most people to avoid this option.

2. **You could keep applying patches or fill the tire up with air, knowing that it will inevitably go flat again.** Some people would choose this option, as it's temporarily the easiest way to go; but, in the end, it's the most expensive choice.

3. **You could attempt to figure out why the tire went flat, replace it with a new and improved tire, and try to avoid whatever caused that flat in the future.** This final solution involves more energy, but it can save you countless hours of worry in the long run. . . . This is the same approach that I feel is appropriate when dealing with relationships. *Ignoring your background will catch up to you.* It may not happen tomorrow or the next day, but it *will* happen.

Our brains erect psychological protection designed to help us get by from day to day. Sometimes these safeguards are extremely helpful, but other times, defenses that once helped us in life just hang around and become poor coping skills. One of the shields I'd like to look at is *denial*. I know the old joke that "it's not just a river in Egypt," but actually, denial can sometimes be really useful. Think about it: If we went through life worrying about all of the potential crises lurking just around the corner, none of us would accomplish anything because we'd be constantly paralyzed with fear. Denial helps us get through the day and allows us to hope that things can change in the future.

However, *denying the past is maladaptive and can lead to unhappiness.* Sure, it would be nice if we could just remember all of the positive things that we learned in the past and forget all of the not-so-nice things, but in reality, our minds don't work that way. All of the positive *and* negative stuff is still somewhere in our brains, impacting us right now as we speak.

Weighing the Scales of Your Life

Let's find out where these old beliefs and feelings about yourself come from. I don't want to bore you with a bunch of neurochemical and psychological theories, but it's important to have an idea about a few very important concepts. For instance, as I touched on in Chapter 11, we all have an "unconscious," which isn't a particular part of the brain, so it can't be pinned down to a specific location—maybe that's why this concept is so difficult for us to comprehend. But it definitely exists, and it makes us act in certain, specific ways.

I see the unconscious as a collection of memories and brain circuits that form out of actual life experiences. From birth on, as our brains develop, we start laying down neural pathways that contain thoughts, emotions, and behaviors. *The more a certain experience happens to us in life, the more ingrained this pathway will be, and the more likely that it will shape the future.* This is an extremely important idea due to the huge ramifications that can occur later in life. Simply stated, *the predominant emotions and behaviors that you see and feel early in life will make a big imprint on your brain.* These experiences define who you are and who you'll be! There's no way around this—significant relationships that involve us (or those close to us) define who we'll become. Our adult personality is the end result of what we received while growing up, including both positive and negative experiences.

Obviously, certain life relationships and occurrences will count more than others. For example, if you got a good grade in school but your parents didn't acknowledge that singular event, it could have left a trace of bitterness. But if you *never* got any recognition or your parents only focused on the negative, this would most likely leave lasting emotional scars. The stage would be set for you to later feel very angry or disconnected from other people, as your experiences would have taught you that others can't or won't give you what you need.

So *one* experience or interaction probably won't have a significant impact on your subsequent relationships. For instance, you may not remember one bad date, but I assure you that the first time you ever got jilted was painful and memorable, and if the connection was long enough or really important to you, your sadness and pain played out over and over in future relationships.

To illustrate this concept, let's suppose that your life is a big set of scales. On one side are all the *positive* things that have happened to you in your life, no matter how petty or great. Conversely, the other side of the scales encompasses all of the *negative* experiences that have happened to you.

The Scales of Life

Clearly, the significant events of your life, as well as those that happen consistently, will weigh heaviest on your scales—so, we can see that something powerful that happens over and over will make one side of the scales quite lopsided. However the scale's tip will determine which set of experiences (positive or negative) drive your current feelings and behaviors.

It makes sense that the way to optimize your happiness would be to have as much of your energy derived from the positive side as possible. Or you could work on understanding the negative side so that you minimize the chance that those experiences become the deciding factor in your relationships and your life. As we systematically analyze important relationships from your past later in the chapter, keep the image of the scales in mind. Our goal is to get that positive side as heavy as we can!

You Become What You've Experienced

As you can see, all of the experiences that constitute your "unconscious" sometimes push forward and cause you to behave in certain ways based on your past. Over the years, I've explained this theory to many people, most of whom initially looked quite surprised. A friend of mine quibbled with me for well over an hour one evening about this very point. He wouldn't concede that a lot of his behaviors were "automatic" and therefore not in his conscious control. I finally drove the point home when I pointed out his need to constantly argue with others over any little thing he disagreed with. His overwhelming need to always be right stemmed from earlier interactions with his parents, and so, arguing was an unconscious pattern for him. He finally came around to my way of thinking, and now he bickers a lot less and has more friends who think he's much less annoying than he used to be.

A simple example clearly illustrates the unconscious: When you move your arm, do you consciously think about the movement before you do it? When you're walking, do you think to yourself, *Left step, right step?* Of course you don't. In a millisecond, your brain automatically makes the connections that allow for these routine behaviors—if you had to think about these movements, your brain would be so cluttered that you wouldn't have time for anything else.

So if our minds are capable of coordinating complex muscles and nerves without conscious thoughts, why wouldn't the same principle apply to your interactions with other people? *We form natural and ingrained ways of dealing with others that will remain unchallenged unless we become aware of these tendencies*—then change can occur.

Memories . . .

It's important to now discuss the most prominent part of our unconscious—the "memory" function—because this will help you sort out which past experiences are valuable to understand, and which ones are probably too insignificant to matter much in the long term.

Memory is defined very strictly: It's a thought pattern of past experiences. What this means is that we can only live as we remember—it does *not* mean that you should only live in the past and not focus on what's happening in the present. But our behaviors and thoughts can only exist because there are memory patterns in our brains that prompt us to be and act in a certain way. This tendency to act through memories is extremely important in the way each one of us forms relationships, chooses life partners, and then gets along in that relationship.

Let me assure you that I'm not asking you to remember everything that's ever happened to you—it's an insurmountable task, and it really wouldn't be all that helpful. Anyway, out of every single experience you've ever had, how much of that could you actually remember and describe in fairly specific detail? I've asked many patients and friends this question, and invariably they'll guess that we remember about 70 to 80 percent of our past experiences. I then challenge them with this question: "Can you even remember most of what you did yesterday?" Usually they lower their guess. We just don't have the capability to have complete visual or auditory recall of the vast majority of our life experiences, and the earlier in life these things occurred, the less we're going to remember.

You simply don't need to remember the very first thing that happened to you in life or rehash every single decision in order to benefit from the therapy in this book. I once met a therapist who, through hypnotic regression, would have patients recall their experience coming down the birth canal so they could relive their own births and regress back to infantile times. Then they'd try to recall every single slight their parents had inflicted upon them. Do I think that any of these patients actually made any progress in their lives? No, because they didn't analyze their major life patterns completely.

Everything I'm going to ask you to do in this chapter is designed to help you understand that *the process of looking at your past patterns must translate to practical knowledge that will help you be happier in a current relationship*. So let's focus on some *themes* and *trends* from your significant past relationships in order to help you understand the problems in your current union.

Meet Your Parents

I'd like to take this opportunity to say a great big public thank you to my parents for setting a good relationship example for me. They've been married for more than 40 years now and are wonderful models for how to cherish and love a partner—I know they certainly shaped my views regarding how two people should treat each other. My parents showed their children what it takes to create a solid relationship that lasts a lifetime, and out of all the things they ever did for me, this was probably one of the most important. I learned from their actions, just as you learned about relationships from *your* parents. (By "parents," I mean your most significant caregivers, whether they were actual biological parents, stepparents, or other relatives.)

Were you as lucky as I was? Did you have parents who knew what it took to maintain their relationship over a lifetime? After all, these were the first adults you saw interacting romantically, so more than likely, you saw their style of fighting, making up, kissing and hugging, struggling, ignoring each other, and dealing with life's problems, and their unspoken message to you came through loud and clear: *This is the way two people in a relationship deal with one another!*

As a child, you were a sponge. You absorbed experiences by just being around your parents. The things that you saw and heard became the norm in your family, and so your parents' relationship has rubbed off on you in ways that you might never have expected. Believe me, I've heard many people tell me their relationship woes and then proudly state, "I'll never end up like my parents!" What they've failed to understand is that *we all end up like our parents, more or less.* The trick is to choose the positive aspects of their relationship to copy and to avoid the inappropriate stuff.

It's relatively easy to see that you shouldn't have a relationship similar to your parents' if it was filled with abuse, rage, or mutual dislike. If they never showed any affection or ended up divorcing, then clearly they had a serious problem that you certainly shouldn't emulate. Yet as we become adults, millions of us go down the same path of pain as our parents did.

However, although we tend to play out roles similar to those of our parents, I've also known people whose parents beat on each other virtually every day for many years, and yet these folks are able to go on to form their own healthy adult relationships and move beyond the disrespect they saw while growing up. Do they have some secret that no one else knows? Absolutely not. They simply understand the importance of systematically analyzing their parents' relationship so that they can avoid making the same mistakes in their own lives.

The bottom line is this: *You'll tend to reenact your parents' relationship with your adult life partners unless you're consciously aware of these parental roles.* I'm going to help you understand the parts your parents played in their relationship. Then, if you realize that you're recreating their roles, you'll be given some different coping skills that may change this dynamic.

First of all, allow me to say that I know it isn't easy to go back in time. After all, childhood was a difficult experience for many people. It was probably especially painful for you if your parents treated you (or each other) poorly. But it's really okay if you attempt to become objective about their treatment of each other and their attitude toward you because your parents aren't gods. Of course we all grow up with a certain reverence and fear of our parents, but at some point, this should be tempered.

The fact is that your parents were just two people who entered a marriage and subsequently found out that they just didn't get along. Or perhaps they even engaged in self-destructive behavior that threatened the very fabric of your family. Maybe they actually did mesh together pretty well but just settled into certain relationship roles—ones that you saw and then copied later on in your life. Whatever the case may have been, I'm now encouraging you to take a look at their relationship because you may learn something about *yourself* in the process.

Let's take a look at some of the more *common roles* that your parents may have exhibited in their relationship, parts you may be playing out later in life.

The Control Freak

Did either your mother or father tend to dominate the other? In many relationships, a pattern is established in which one person assumes the controlling role and the other takes on that of the passive victim. Usually this breaks down to dominant male/submissive female, as many times the dynamic is based strictly on finances (the breadwinner of the house is set up to be the decision-maker), but females can be just as controlling as men. Either way, the result is an unequal power base between the partners, with one person (the controller) appearing stronger while the other person appears weaker.

One of the motivators behind the controlling personality is a need to make all decisions and tell others what *will* be done. This person will frequently criticize and judge their partner—nothing is ever quite right, and their partner has to constantly be on the defensive. The controller often gets their way due to sheer intimidation; unfortunately, this leads to their partner living in fear of the consequences if the rules aren't followed. The controller usually has a great capacity to explode in anger if things aren't done to his or her satisfaction. The end result is that the passive partner gives up any sense of independent thinking and lives to "please."

Have you committed to a relationship where you took on the characteristics of your controlling parent, or became a victim just like your submissive parent? If so, the solution is this: You and your partner need to respect each other's opinions and *compromise*. No one person should be getting their own way all the time. Realize that *a healthy relationship allows for both partners to be in control at different times*.

The Immature Parent

Just because someone is an adult doesn't mean that they'll necessarily act like one! Did one (or both) of your parents act out in an immature fashion and always seem to be in a crisis? This category includes parents who threw temper tantrums, abused substances, and acted selfishly— they simply never wanted to take responsibility for their actions or for the family. They may have had trouble with money, holding down a job, or staying faithful; or perhaps it was difficult for them to spend any sort of quality time with you. So, in order for the family system to stabilize, the other parent invariably had to pick up the slack and become super-responsible. It's possible that *you* may have even felt as if you were more like a parent than your mother or father was.

Immature parents often aren't forced to confront their issue because they give the impression that they'll crumble and get even worse if challenged. It seems as if they're fragile, unstable, and on the edge. There's constantly a problem getting in the way of the immature person's happiness, and family interactions center on putting out their fires rather than on spending worthwhile time together.

Have you committed to a relationship in which you took on the characteristics of an irresponsible, immature parent and needed "help" from your partner frequently? Or are you involved with someone who needs you to constantly stabilize their bad behavior and moods? If so, the solution is this: Realize that *for a relationship to be successful, both people must behave in responsible, adult ways*. Both should be able to count on their needs getting met—the relationship shouldn't revolve around the chaotic demands of one unstable individual.

The Withholder

Some people have great difficulty expressing love and affection to others, for a variety of reasons. When they commit to a serious relationship, their system essentially shuts down, and they become distant and uninvolved with their partner. Perhaps it's too scary for them to achieve a significant level of intimacy, or maybe they only feel wanted when they force their partner to "come and get them." Either way, their partner is left frustrated and will repeatedly attempt to get them to "open up."

Did your parents show affection to each other, or was there a wall between them? Some people grow up never seeing their parents embracing or acting as if they love each other. Usually the parent who does desire the affection feels abandoned and rejected and sometimes just gives up, and there can be arguments about sex—and even divorce—if the distance becomes too great.

Have you committed to a relationship in which you took on the characteristics of a distant and uninvolved parent who had trouble showing affection? Or have you chosen partners who were emotional "projects," unable to open up and give you the necessary level of intimacy and connection? If so, the solution is this: *Understand that for two people to thrive in a relationship, there has to be a spirit of cooperation, and the willingness to communicate. Both* partners need to be inclined to give a reasonable amount of affection and be vulnerable to each other. They should see that it's *not* threatening to share fears and dreams; after all, healthy relationships exist because both people are in it *all the way*—they're not just going through the motions with one foot out the door.

The Complainer

It's amazing that some people who seemingly despise each other will stay together for years. It's as if they feed off of each other's negativity and set up passive-aggressive cycles of behavior. It's always the case that one or the other isn't quite "getting enough" of something, and they complain—loudly—that their needs aren't being met. And these people have children who get to watch their parents constantly bickering.

At the root of all of this whining are the complainers who feel as if the world should be a certain way. They seem to have a set of rules about relationships that everyone else should automatically know and follow. When this doesn't happen, the complainer will try to verbally hammer their partner into making everything right. The cycle goes around and around, with the complainer never satisfied and the partner feeling helpless, as if they can never do anything right.

I'm sure that you heard your parents complain about each other occasionally, but was this one of their main ways of interacting? Did one (or both) of your parents yell a lot about insignificant matters, never seeming content with life? And have you consequently committed to a relationship in which you took on the characteristics of a complaining, dissatisfied parent? Or have you chosen partners who make you feel that you're never doing enough for them? If so, your solution is this: Realize that a complainer is really just trying to make their partner feel as unhappy inside as they do. Ironically, a complainer gets the upper hand because their partner is always on the defensive and trying to do things just right. *Accept the fact that complaining and negativity won't get you anywhere.*

Parents Who Divorce

The numbers aren't pretty: Millions of parents get divorced each year. I hope that you aren't a product of a broken family, but I know that the odds are fairly high that you are. If you had the experience of seeing your parents go through the pain of a divorce—even if things went smoothly and you weren't thrust in the middle of their disagreements—you were affected by it. There's no way around it: The process of divorce takes its toll on children. They're being shuttled back and forth between two parents and two houses—if they're lucky. Some kids hardly ever get to see one of the parents again. It doesn't matter if your parents stayed together but fought constantly, or if they went ahead and got a divorce—either way, they did you no favors. It's pretty straightforward—you see your parents utilizing poor coping skills with each other, so you miss out on the opportunity to be taught what it takes to maintain a fulfilling relationship. You're not necessarily destined to repeat your parents' pattern, but you'll probably have to work harder to define the critical aspects of a satisfying, lifelong relationship.

Did your parents set a good example of how two people in a relationship should treat each other? If they didn't, they've thrown you into the game without the proper equipment. The solution is this: *If your parents couldn't keep their act together, you'll need to objectively analyze the weaknesses in their relationship so that you don't repeat their same mistakes.* Ask yourself what they did wrong. What were the mistakes they made? What could they have done differently?

A final thought for children of divorce: You must let go of the resentment you harbor toward your parents for breaking up your family, since that bitterness will only make it more likely that you'll follow in their footsteps. Also, do whatever is necessary to educate yourself about qualities of healthy relationships, whether you do this by entering counseling or a support group, or just reading a few well-chosen self-help books.

With a lot of hard work and introspection, *anyone* can overcome their natural tendency to end up like their parents.

Your Relationship with Your Parents

There's *another* important childhood experience that will affect the way you handle your adult relationships—in fact, it may be more crucial than your parents' relationship with each other. The next part of this chapter will be spent focusing on your parents' relationship with *you*. After all, this was the first major relationship you were involved in, albeit not of your own choice—you got what you got in the parent category, whether you liked it or not. However, this relationship has had a powerful impact on your future relationship decisions and choice of life partners.

I understand that it's tempting to discount these past experiences, especially if things didn't go so well with your parents, but I hope that you'll make an effort to understand your dynamic with them because if you don't, it will still be there. I wish that there were a simpler way, but there isn't. The reality is this: *You also tend to recreate your relationship with your parents unless you become consciously aware of your childhood role.* Put another way, you may tend to find partners that allow you to go back in time and relive some of those old emotions and past parent-child interactions.

In practical terms, how does this happen? There are two ways that this plays out in your intimate relationships:

1. *You take the role you had as a child.* That is, you choose someone to fill your parent's role.

2. *You take the role of your parent.* You choose someone who's like you were as a child.

In the first scenario, you simply stay in the role you had as a child because it's familiar. You bond with a partner who acts just like your parent. Unfortunately, if this relationship wasn't satisfying for you as a child, it's certainly not going to change for the better now that you're an adult. If your partner treats you in the same way you were treated while growing up, then you have an unequal balance of power, for instead of both of you behaving in adult roles, they become the parent and you're the child.

In the second scenario, you've strongly identified with your parent and take on their personality characteristics when you interact with your partner. You go about putting your partner in exactly the same position you were in while growing up. You become your mother or father, and your partner plays the role you had as a child—once again, this relationship is unbalanced as far as power goes.

I know that this concept sounds complicated, but it's really not. Just ask yourself, "Did I marry my mother or father?" or "Have I become like my mother or father with my partner?" These are essential questions for you to consider in any relationship, because you could absolutely ruin your chances of relationship success if you set up old situations that didn't work then.

Let's now attempt to categorize the role that you played with your parents so that if you recognize that you're recreating some parent-child interactions with your partner, you can begin the process of developing better coping skills.

I know that there are a million different ways to raise children. Your parents surely had their own unique theories about raising you, and if they were really smart, they recognized that their relationship with you would determine a lot about your success in adult love relationships.

What You Should Have Received from Your Parents

To ensure your future success, your parents should have given you some of the following gifts:

- First and foremost, they should have made you feel **safe at home.**

- They should have made you feel **secure enough to share your feelings** with them, without undue criticism or judgment.

- They should have helped you develop the **skills to solve life problems on your own** without taking care of them for you. Allowing you to make decisions and deal with the aftermath is an important parental job.

- They should have **told you when they were wrong** or made mistakes in dealing with you.

- They should have **allowed you to pick and choose** your own school activities and friends.

- They should have **let you be a kid**—that is, they shouldn't have forced you to take on adult responsibilities before you were ready.

- They **shouldn't have blamed you for their marital issues.** You shouldn't have been placed in a position of choosing one parent over another.

- They shouldn't have berated each other in front of you. Likewise, they **shouldn't have verbally or physically abused you.**

- They should have had a **firm but clearly defined set of rules** for you. Their rewards and punishments should have been consistent and fair, so you knew what to expect from them.

- They should have **spent time with you, teaching and listening.** They should have made you feel that they were in your corner when you tried something new.

Your parents should have followed these principles, not only because it's the right thing to do, but because the qualities listed above set an example of how a healthy relationship develops. I don't expect that you received every single one of these gifts, but for each one that was lacking in your childhood, it represents more of an uphill climb for you to know what a good relationship entails.

Stop Acting Like a Child

Unfortunately, a lot of people didn't get great parents—they were subject to caretakers who had their own baggage and problems that played out within the family unit. It's a sad fact that some parents just aren't very good at doing the right thing to raise a child properly. Most of the damage they cause their children is easy to spot, but the real wounds are deep, lasting . . . and invisible.

Inadequate parents can't teach their children how to have good relationships because they don't know themselves. Therefore, their children grow up repeating old, familiar roles because it's all *they* know. *Show me someone who's failed at several relationships, and I'll show you someone who's playing out old roles from childhood without even knowing it.*

Here are some of the more unhealthy roles from childhood that a person could recreate in an adult relationship. Do any of these look familiar to you?

The Abandoned Child

I sincerely hope that you weren't abandoned by your parents. I'm not even talking about the extreme case in which a baby is left on a doorstep somewhere. Abandonment usually takes on more subtle forms, both physically and emotionally. It's truly one of the most frightening situations any child could ever face. Abandonment means *neglect*. Did you grow up always feeling as if you wanted more of something from your parents but you couldn't get it?

The opposite of abandonment is *attention*, which is something every child craves. If you didn't get it, or you just didn't feel any real positive connection to your parents, this will play out later in life with you either becoming involved with someone who abandons you, just like your parents did, or you'll do the abandoning, withdrawing your love and putting up walls in the relationship. You'll either feel neglected by your partner or you'll neglect them back—one way or another, it spells relationship disaster.

So, if you felt disconnected as a child from your parents, you'll likely seek out (unconsciously) partners who can't relate well because it's what you know from your past. Ask yourself if you've had relationships where you constantly felt neglected or always wished that you could get more from your partner. If so, it may be that you're choosing partners who lack the ability to connect, just like one or both of your parents. You become the abandoned child, and your partner is the neglectful parent. Or are *you* the partner who withdraws, just like your parent did with you? Do you act as if your partner will leave at any time? Does your brain tell you that since it happened before, it could certainly happen again? If so, the solution is this: *Overcome the abandonment.* Realize that for a successful relationship, both people need to feel wanted and cherished. Work on interacting with your partner, and notice that it really isn't scary to become closer and more intimate—no one is left feeling neglected or insignificant.

The Spoiled Child

The opposite end of the spectrum from the abandoned child are the kids whose parents make them the center of the universe. Taken to the extreme, this becomes *overindulgent*, so what emerges later in life is someone who demands that everyone else treat them as their parents did. A lot of demanding adults have simply been raised with an "I'll get what I want when I want it" attitude. What's interesting here is that most of these people have actually felt trapped and smothered for most of their lives and consequently don't develop a sense of compromise and fairness. They expect relationship partners to cater to them, and when something disappointing occurs, there's usually a substantial amount of anger.

For instance, I know a woman who has chosen partners based on how many presents they'll give her. She likes to be the center of attention, but she can never get enough, so her suitors eventually tire of this and move on. She rationalizes that none of these men are "good enough" and fails to see that she's really just repeating a pattern she fell into with one of her parents years ago.

On the other hand, some people will make their partner the solitary focus of everything in their life, and sometimes they become insanely jealous if their mate tries to develop separate interests. They've become the smothering parents, and their partner is the child needing all the attention.

This role can therefore be defined like this: The spoiled children will remain spoiled and form relationships with those who will lavish them with attention; or they'll tend to spoil their partners, sometimes to an annoying degree.

Ask yourself if you fit the profile of a person who must have their way all of the time. Are you a compromiser, or are you just plain stubborn? Have you felt as if your partner could never please you enough, even with considerable effort? Have you chosen partners who tend to overindulge you, but then cross the line and eventually make you feel trapped in the relationship? Or have you made your partner the center of your world to the exclusion of family, friends, and outside activities? If so, the solution is this: *Overcome the tendency to overindulge.* Realize that for a successful relationship to flourish, both people must get pampered equally. A healthy relationship involves give-*and*-take, with neither partner receiving a lot more of anything than the other one does.

The Scapegoat

In some dysfunctional families, the child gets the blame for anything and everything. I recently watched a disturbing documentary on TV that showed two teenage boys being berated and abused by their mother, who blamed them for everything that went wrong with her or the family. I could see the few ounces of self-esteem the boys had seeping away right before my very eyes, and I found myself wondering how they could possibly ever grow up to have healthy relationships.

Did you have to take the blame for your parents' issues? If so, you may have felt inferior and ashamed of yourself for no good reason. Many people have been subjected to unwarranted criticism in their childhoods—ask yourself if you've tended to choose partners who make you feel inferior. If you have, then the solution is this: *Overcome the blame game.* Understand that two people who blame each other for relationship issues will most likely be partners who are going to be breaking up soon. No one is *solely* to blame when things get tough. It's time for you and your partner to both shoulder the burden for relationship mistakes. Don't allow yourself (or your partner!) to take all of the responsibility for problems.

The Child Who Grows Up Too Quickly

Sometimes a parent is lost through death or divorce, and the remaining caretaker is left to raise the children and often feels overwhelmed. So one of the children may be forced into a position of taking on adult responsibilities before they're ready. For instance, I know of some 12- and

13-year-olds who have had to raise their younger siblings.

You may feel that developing some adult-coping skills as a child is an okay idea, but the problem is that a kid must also be allowed to be a kid. Becoming a little adult blends the roles of parent and child, so in the midst of a chaotic home situation, the child has to become a rescuer, dealing with difficult situations in a responsible way. The same role is played out in later relationships.

Look at your relationships and decide if you've chosen irresponsible partners who do nothing or are lazy. If so, do you assume that old role of saving the day, and get all the accolades for having your act together? Or, on the other hand, have you forced partners into the role of taking charge while you assume a dependent position? The solution is: *Overcome the rescuer-victim mentality*. It's simply not your job to pick up the slack for a passive partner, not is it their job to do it for you. A relationship based on a rescue mission is one that will probably fail.

The Controlled Child

Some parents have the need to treat their children like little puppets. They make all of the decisions for the kids, from the clothes they wear to the friends they choose, and the children are expected to obey and carry out orders like good soldiers. This is sad, because children need to be taught how to think for themselves. This childhood role easily translates into an adult who can't make reasonable independent decisions and who searches for a parental figure to take charge, for they've learned that, in a relationship, there's always an element of control present.

Did your parents allow you to do your own thing? Or did you grow up being afraid to speak your mind? Ask yourself if you've tended to choose partners who dominated you, or if you've turned the tables and tried to give them a taste of the medicine that you had to swallow. If so, the solution is this: *Overcome the power struggles.* If you've been pushed around, ask yourself if this is the way you really want to live. *Realize that an unequal balance of power in your relationship can be potentially devastating.* Form a relationship based on mutual respect, in which both partners are allowed to take the lead occasionally. There shouldn't be a leader and a follower, but two equal people who aren't scared to speak up and take control once in a while.

What Are Your Relationship Roles?

It's worth the effort to generally define your *relationship roles* (as well as your partner's). Even if you're engaged in a mutually satisfying partnership, this **exercise** can be tremendously helpful in strengthening your bond.

Take out a pen and a piece of paper and make two columns. In the first one, I'd like you to define the roles that you sometimes take in your relationships. You can get started by finishing this statement: "I'm a _____ in the relationship." For example, is there one particular role that you naturally assume with a partner? Also remember that there are positive and negative aspects to any role. For example, if you answer, "I'm a *giver* in the relationship," you also need to ask yourself whether you sometimes give *too much* . . . to the exclusion of your own needs.

In the next column, complete this sentence: "My parents saw me as a _____ as a child." You may be amazed at some of the similarities between the old roles you played as a child and the ones you're playing today.

It's my hope that this exercise (and this chapter) have helped you understand why you've chosen certain partners and types of people in your relationships. Each one of us has a characteristic way of interacting with our partners, and this is based on our past. Your chances of forming a healthy relationship can only improve if you're able to move beyond those old childhood roles to new ways of relating that fit the adult you are today.

CHAPTER 21

The Relationship
That Lasts a Lifetime

A FTER ALL OF OUR HARD WORK SIFTING THROUGH THE sands of the past, it's now time to live in the present. The real quality of your personal relationships will depend on the effort you exert *right now*—I'm talking about *today*, not yesterday or three days from now! I know that it's easy to get caught up in the daily grind of working, raising children, paying bills, and focusing on anything else *but* your relationship . . . yet when it's all said and done, what will matter most to you won't be how many hours of overtime you worked or how much stuff you accumulated. No, the greatest joy in your life will be remembered through your relationships—the quality of which can only exist through your actions as you live life on a *daily* basis. What you were planning to do for your partner in the future doesn't count for much. *The only way for your relationship to be successful is for you to make it successful— every single moment of every single day.*

It may seem like a tall order to fill, but why would you be in a relationship in the first place if you didn't want to make it great? Many people forget this idea since they're too busy wallowing in negativity. It's too late when they realize that they forgot to do the little things that separate an outstanding relationship from a mediocre one. They end up regretting the fact that they failed to really connect with their partner in a loving and positive way.

I can't believe that anybody enters a relationship hoping that unpleasant things will happen, but for many couples, a sense of neglect does set in, as day by day, the negatives chip away at the relationship, until there's nothing left at all. People usually aren't even aware that the relationship ended because of their daily disregard— which is sad because it's a condition that's so easy to reverse.

So start bettering your relationship right now by answering the question, "How do I live for *today* in my relationship?"

Practice Gratitude

I can clearly remember the day that I came home from work feeling beleaguered and exhausted after dealing with several difficult patients. I was in no mood to expend energy on my relationship with my wife, and since I *was* in the mood to complain and feel sorry for myself, the night was shaping up to be a real downer for us both. . . . Then something wonderful happened.

When I walked into the kitchen, I saw a piece of paper lying on the counter, addressed to me in my wife's handwriting. I opened it up, and inside was one of the nicest gestures anyone has ever directed toward me. Betsy had composed a list of things in our relationship for which she was *grateful*. Most of what she had listed were actions that I simply performed in the relationship without ever really being aware of their impact on her—after all, my parents taught me that two people should just be nice to each other in a relationship. But I had forgotten that some people *aren't* very nice to their partners, and Betsy let me know that she didn't take that fact (or me) for granted.

This list was probably one of the most important presents that we've ever shared. My wife had taken an active step to focus on the positives in our marriage, instead of dwelling on the things we lacked. Moreover, she made me feel good about myself. She took the time to actually think about us and communicated the words that couples normally don't say to each other. She didn't wait for some "special day" in the future to tell me how she felt—our day was *now*.

One of the challenges of living in the present is seeing the favorable aspects of your relationship. *You need to begin the process of expressing gratitude for anything that's good between you and your partner.* Don't wait until special occasions such as birthdays and anniversaries, when you write out the perfunctory card—make your relationship thrive by acknowledging your partner's efforts *often*. Why should you do this? The answer is simple: You don't know if your loved one will be around tomorrow! This sounds morbid, but I mean it as a jolt of reality. I've counseled many an individual whose partner was suddenly and tragically taken away in an instant—a deep sense of regret remained with these people forever because they realized that the time to say all of those loving words had passed.

The opposite of relationship gratitude is relationship *neglect*. Most unions crumble because the partners fell into a pattern of *existing*, and not truly *living*, with each other. To exist with another person, you don't really have to do anything except physically be there. But living with someone is an entirely different matter. Living is an *active* process, done each and every day. It's not enough to just get by without any major relationship conflicts—that's only the starting point.

Be very clear on this point, because this concept is vitally important to understand: *Dealing with your occasional disagreements is only the first step for you and your significant other.* This is just the foundation you will build upon. For example, many couples know how to take care of relationship crises, but they don't seem to know how to deal with each other in between. They practice disregard on a daily basis but spring into action when a calamity happens. These couples are missing the point that their energy should be spent on the *positives* in the relationship, not wasted on crisis management. I assure you that there will always be problems in any relationship—no matter how hard you try to eliminate them—but it's actually more difficult to connect with your partner through all of the positive things you have together. Relationship neglect occurs when you don't give thanks for all of the great qualities your partner brings to the table—and no amount of comfort and therapy can take away so many years of oversight. That's why it's important to enjoy and appreciate your partner *today*, in the here-and-now.

The Relationship Pyramid

How can you move to a more grateful and appreciative attitude toward your partner? Take a look at *the relationship pyramid*, which illustrates a hierarchy of priorities that must be accomplished for your relationship to flourish. (The top is the most rewarding, and therefore most important, level.)

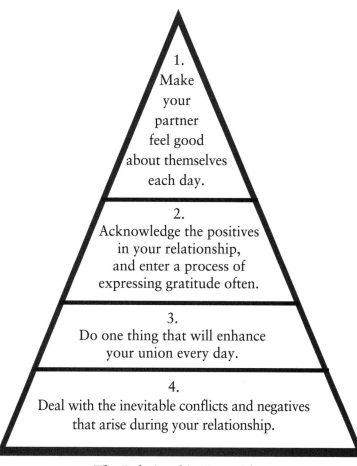

1.
Make
your
partner
feel good
about themselves
each day.

2.
Acknowledge the positives
in your relationship,
and enter a process of
expressing gratitude often.

3.
Do one thing that will enhance
your union every day.

4.
Deal with the inevitable conflicts and negatives
that arise during your relationship.

The Relationship Pyramid

When most people first see this pyramid, they think that it's upside down, since they've come to believe that working through relationship struggles is their top priority. The exact opposite is true—the critical level is the top one, because if this is embraced as a relationship must, then every other level will naturally flow just right. For example, if your top priority is to make your partner feel good about who they are, then the potential for relationship conflicts will be greatly minimized. Let's quickly analyze the top three levels, since these are concerned with building a positive relationship.

Level 1

Make your partner feel good about themselves each day. I know of no more worthwhile ideal in any love relationship. This thought should be in the back of your mind every single day that you're with your partner. You should be doing this simply because it's the right thing to do. I challenge you to ask yourself each day, "What can I do to make my partner feel good and enhance their self-esteem?" It doesn't matter if it's a small gesture, such as paying a compliment, or if it's something grand that makes a lifelong dream come true. There's something positive you can give to your partner each and every day, even if it's as simple as articulating how happy and secure you feel in the relationship. Openly expressing your love every day is a good start.

Level 2

Acknowledge the positives, and express gratitude often. When your expectations aren't met, it's easy to fall into the rut of dwelling only on disappointments and frustrations. But if you do this, then I can virtually guarantee a terrible relationship experience.

You can make a significant change in your relationship (and your internal sense of contentment) if you begin to focus on the pleasant qualities and contributions from your partner instead. Don't forget—people need to feel valued and recognized for their efforts, so expressing gratitude will also go a long way toward ensuring that the good stuff will keep on coming. It's indeed true that in order to receive positive energy, you must first put out *your own* positive energy.

Level 3

Do one good deed every day for your partner. This one speaks for itself. Make a promise to yourself right now that you'll adopt this as a rule of daily living. I don't care if you're arguing and you're both so mad at each other that you can't see straight—in fact, that may be the very best time to act in a kind way toward each other. Perhaps that day's good deed could be to admit that you were wrong and ask for forgiveness. After all, do you really want to be the kind of person who treats another human being poorly?

Be Curious about Your Partner

In addition to the top three levels of the relationship pyramid, all successful relationships have something else in common: Both partners exhibit a healthy interest in learning about each other. If you and your partner took a quiz about each other, there's a reasonable chance that you'd fail because many people are so involved in other activities that communication with their mate suffers.

Ask yourself if you know what your partner *really* thinks about life. I know it sounds kind of silly, like a bad first-date question, to ask your partner, "Hey, what do you want out of life?" But why shouldn't you know (or want to find out) what they really want and need? If you're thinking about being with someone for the next 50 years or so, shouldn't you be able to share your fears, dreams, joys, and disappointments with each other? Research indicates that couples only talk to each other a few minutes a day on average. I think that's a shame. If you're truly afraid to share your innermost thoughts and insecurities with someone, then you should probably ask yourself if this is indeed the right person for *you*.

If you don't attempt to share your fears and hopes with your partner, then you're always going to feel somewhat alone, even though you're technically in a relationship. Don't you want to know about all of the accomplishments and losses that your partner has been through? My wife and I have related much of the details of our childhood experiences and have really opened up to each other. Of course I felt incredibly vulnerable at first, but the support and understanding I received from her has made us even closer. You just may be pleasantly surprised by the amount of empathy and support you could receive if you just let your partner inside, for sharing promotes closeness and intimacy; while withdrawing only makes it easier for you both to be indifferent about the relationship.

Yes, this is a vulnerable experience, and I understand that you or your partner may be the type of person who has trouble talking about your life. If this is the case, it may be easier to write up a *personal history*. This is something that I direct most of my patients to do so that they can have some perspective on their life thus far. Once you start writing, you may be surprised to learn that it can be a cathartic experience, almost like a release of pent-up energy.

Write about the major themes in your life—the most important of which are the *losses* that you've experienced, because *personal losses affect the quality of relationships*. There's no way around this. Every loss that you haven't processed can only make it more difficult to form satisfying, intimate unions in the future. It's as if each loss adds another layer to a suit of armor that you wear. At some point, you'll withdraw into your armor and find it nearly impossible to form relationships at all because you'll be afraid to lose yet another person. Ironically, your fear of more losses makes it more likely that you *will* lose a great relationship because you were unable to open up to your partner.

Have you lost relationships with people whom you really loved? If so, celebrate that you're still standing and have the courage to enter a new relationship. *Losses are intensely painful, but they don't have to destroy your potential to form bonds with others. Instead, loss can be viewed as the stuff that makes you a unique person.*

Accept Vulnerability

You inherit a risk of vulnerability each time you get involved with another person. When you begin to share feelings and invest time into a relationship, you're taking a big chance that you may get hurt or things may not work out and you may end up alone again. There's no guarantee when it comes to affairs of the heart, so you have a choice. You can either avoid any and all intimate relationships because you're scared of being hurt or rejected, or you can just accept that this may possibly happen to you. Sure, you take a chance of being hurt, but who says that it will definitely end up that way? Instead, you might find the love of your life. Just because you give someone else the power to hurt you doesn't mean that they *will*. After all, you have the power to hurt them, also. It's a delicate road that you'll both navigate, but I can't think of many things that are worthwhile that don't contain some element of risk or vulnerability. There's nothing inherently wrong with sharing fears and insecurities (and hopes and dreams) with another human being; in fact, it's a freeing experience. Try trusting your partner and opening up to them, and encourage them to do the same with you. Chances are, you'll be amazed by the results.

Promote Tolerance

I'm going to state something rather obvious here: Your partner will sometimes make you very angry, and you, in turn, will upset your partner. A perfect relationship doesn't exist, and if it did, it would probably be too boring to keep you interested for very long.

Your life relationships can only be *managed*, not conformed into the precise shape that you desire. This is a hard lesson for most of us to learn, because we instinctively want our partners to do what *we* think is best, for we're right and they're wrong. I'm sure that at some point, you've caught yourself wondering, *Why can't my partner just think like I do?*

Well, I'll tell you why: *They're a completely different person, with different motivations, values, and interests!* If you wanted a clone, you should have married yourself. The only way I know for you to muddle through a relationship and keep your sanity is to accept the fact that your partner will have different priorities from you.

So how do we become tolerant? I'll admit that it isn't easy. After all, intolerance is one of the main reasons why entire nations have fought each other over the centuries. Tolerance implies that you accept the inevitable differences that exist between any two people. Instead of yelling, "Pick up your shoes! Why can't you put them away like I do?" you could say it a better way: "It's really important to me to have a neat house—would you please put away your shoes?" In the second sentence, you recognize that you and your partner place a different importance on this issue, but you still ask for an adjustment in behavior. If your partner tells you "Forget it!" then the problem is with *their* intolerance.

And once again, don't forget how important empathy is. Couples who stay together exhibit a willingness to see things from their partner's point of view.

Know What Really Matters

Successful couples also have something else in common: They have the sense to focus on the really *important* issues in their relationship, and they don't spend time on trivial matters that won't mean a thing years from now. They pick and choose their battles—and sometimes even let things go completely—for the sake of their relationship.

This concept goes hand-in-hand with tolerance, and I can't stress how important it is. After all, you and your partner are going to have habits that drive each other crazy once in a while, but your union should ultimately be grounded in more important principles such as *love, community,* and *spirituality.* The need to treat your partner with *kindness* and *respect* should absolutely override your wish to have every little thing go your particular way.

Think about it: Many years from now, you probably won't remember who won the most arguments or who got their way most often. What you *will* remember is that your relationship gave a deeper meaning to your and your partner's life. So, whenever you're ready to say something that will potentially damage your relationship, I'd like you to ponder these four words: *Is it worth it?* Then ask yourself: *Is it really worth the complaint, or walking around in a bad mood? Is it worth yelling at the person I love? Will this issue matter five years down the road? Or can I focus on all of the good things I have in my life and my relationship?*

What I'm really saying is that we're all on this planet for a very short time, so if you have the choice, why not try to fill up every second of that time with love and joy?

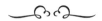

Afterword

Y OU'VE DONE IT! YOU AND I HAVE ALMOST FINISHED OUR time together—yet I hope that our connection won't be severed completely, for there still may be some work to do. I wrote *A Relationship for a Lifetime* to be a comprehensive resource that you can use over and over again for years to come. I'll wager that you will learn something new each time you refer back to this book or share it with your partner and friends.

The relationship concepts that we've discussed in these pages are *timeless* and apply to everyone. Let's face it— the creation of a great relationship is no easy task, and it never hurts to have a little bit of luck on your side. However, you can greatly increase your odds if you're willing to continue on a journey of introspection and understanding. I know that perhaps it was a bold claim to state that this is *"everything* you need to know to create a love that lasts," but my belief is that I've spoken the truth about relationship dynamics and affairs of the heart. After all, you deserve nothing less.

Gimmicks and game-playing in your personal relationships won't work for you in the long term. What *will* make a difference in your life is an unrelenting focus on an *understanding* of your relationship choices, as well as a *demand* that your partner treat you with the utmost respect and dignity each and every day. No matter what struggles you've been through up until this point in time—you have an undeniable right to pursue happiness with a partner who lives to make you happy.

When you look back at your life many years from now, you'll invariably judge the quality of your experiences by the *people* whom you let into your world. Many of us learn too late that material possessions ultimately don't count for much, but our *relationships* are life's most important creations. So it certainly would be a shame if you went through life with an empty feeling about them because you never had a chance to learn *real* concepts that have a fighting chance of improving both your partnerships *and* you as a person.

Think of this book as that chance. I know that I've presented a tremendous amount of information that may seem overwhelming to put into practice in your everyday life. But don't give up, even if you're in a difficult relationship right now, or just haven't connected with the right person yet. Contrary to what we keep hearing about the high rate of relationship failures, outstanding relationships *do* exist, and the people who form these wonderful connections aren't any different from you or me! You now have the tools to create a satisfying, lasting relationship, or enhance the one you already have.

Looking back, I'd like to think that *A Relationship for a Lifetime* is ultimately about the most important relationship of all—the one you have with *you!* After all, the only way to contribute positively to *any* relationship with another human being is to first *make peace with yourself.* Your primary goal in life should be to make yourself the best person you can be, because a balanced, healthy, fulfilling relationship can only arise from a contented person who brings positive energy to the world.

Good luck in your continuing search for happiness, and God bless you!

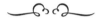

About the Author

Kelly E. Johnson, M.D., is a nationally recognized psychiatrist and relationship therapist. He has extensive media experience, having appeared regularly on television shows such as *The Jenny Jones Show* and *Montel* as their "relationship expert."

Dr. Johnson's radio show, *Private Lives,* has been based in Chicago for the past decade and is geared toward helping people solve their most difficult relationship, health, and emotional problems. In addition to winning many broadcast awards, this show has consistently been rated the number-one radio talk show on Sunday nights.

Since receiving his degree in psychiatry from Northwestern University, Dr. Johnson has maintained a private consultation practice. He lives with his wife, Betsy, and their two dogs in Chicago. Website: **www.DrKellyJohnson.net**

Notes

Notes

Notes

Notes

Notes

Notes

We hope you enjoyed this Hay House book. If you would like to receive a free catalog featuring additional Hay House books and products, or if you would like information about the Hay Foundation, please contact:

Hay House, Inc.
P.O. Box 5100
Carlsbad, CA 92018-5100

(760) 431-7695 or (800) 654-5126
(760) 431-6948 (fax) or (800) 650-5115 (fax)
www.hayhouse.com

Published and distributed in Australia by:
Hay House Australia Pty. Ltd. • 18/36 Ralph St.
Alexandria NSW 2015
Phone: 612-9669-4299 • *Fax:* 612-9669-4144 • www.hayhouse.com.au

Published and distributed in the United Kingdom by:
Hay House UK, Ltd. • Unit 62, Canalot Studios
222 Kensal Rd., London W10 5BN • *Phone:* 44-20-8962-1230
Fax: 44-20-8962-1239 • www.hayhouse.co.uk

Published and distributed in the Republic of South Africa by:
Hay House SA (Pty), Ltd., P.O. Box 990, Witkoppen 2068
Phone/Fax: 27-11-706-6612 • orders@psdprom.co.za

Distributed in Canada by:
Raincoast • 9050 Shaughnessy St., Vancouver, B.C. V6P 6E5
Phone: (604) 323-7100 • *Fax:* (604) 323-2600

Sign up via the Hay House USA Website to receive the Hay House online newsletter and stay informed about what's going on with your favorite authors. You'll receive bimonthly announcements about: Discounts and Offers, Special Events, Product Highlights, Free Excerpts, Giveaways, and more!
www.hayhouse.com